DEVELOPMENT AND CONTESTATIONS IN INDIA

INSIGHTS FROM ODISHA

DEVELOPMENT AND CONTESTATIONS IN INDIA

INSIGHTS FROM ODISHA

Seema Mallik

ABHIJEET PUBLCATIONS
NEW DELHI 110002

ABHIJEET PUBLICATIONS
4658-A, First Floor, Ambika Bhawan,
21 Ansari Road, New Delhi 110002
Phone: 011-23259444
E-mail: abhijeetpublication@gmail.com
www.abhijeetpublications.com

DEVELOPMENT AND CONTESTATIONS IN INDIA: INSIGHTS FROM ODISHA

First Published 2020

ISBN 978-93-88865-46-3

PRINTED IN INDIA

Published by J.K. Singh for Abhijeet Publications, New Delhi-110002, Lasertypeset by Abhijeet Typesetters, New Delhi and Printed at Dynamic Printers, New Delhi.

Dedicated
to the loving memory of
my parents

Acknowledgements

This book is a revised version of a UGC Major Research Project 'Development and Conflict: Insights from Odisha' supported by University Grants Commission (UGC) New Delhi. At the outset, I extend my heartfelt gratitude to UGC New Delhi for giving me an opportunity to delve into a subject very dear to me. I also thank Utkal University, Bhubaneswar for facilitating the study. A special thanks to the Department of Political Science Utkal University and all my colleagues for their support.

I would particularly like to thank Dr. Rosanne Ruten and Dr. Gerben Noothboom of the *Moving Matters Group*, University of Amsterdam, for their new ideas and valuable criticisms of earlier versions of the work. I am also thankful to Prof Pralay Kanungo (Centre for Political Studies, Jawaharlal Nehru University, New Delhi) and Prof. Madhushree Sekher, Tata Institute of Social Sciences (TISS) Mumbai, for their generous suggestions which have helped shape this volume.

I am also most grateful to the local support that I received during my area visits to Posco site, Kalinganagar and Vedanta. Without this support from both the government and non-government sources this study would have not been possible. I received the cooperation of both pro-Posco and anti-Posco activists which has facilitated my understanding of the conflict. I need to offer special thanks to local villagers and the panchayat office who helped me perceive the ongoing agitations and resistance. A special thanks to my student Tanmay Swain and his family from Dhinkia village which is the nerve centre of the agitation. From them, I received first hand insights into the lucrative *pan leaves* cultivation and business which is the chief livelihood of the region. I also express my gratitude to the rehabilitation colonies of Kalinganagar and Vedanta for sharing their experiences. I also had an opportunity to interact with several Tata and Vedanta officials at the site.

No words can express my gratitude to the *dongoria kondhos*, the tribal inhabitants of Niyamgiri hills, at Lanjigarh. Although, very shy and non-communicative with strangers, the *dongorias* particularly women gave valuable information on their lives, livelihood and resistance to Vedanta. I also am indebted to the *kutia kondhas* residing at the foothills of the hills, in the rehabilitation colony. My special thanks to the Corporate Social Responsibility (CSR), Vedanta Alumina Limited, Lanjigarh Kalahandi district for their cooperation and help.

I am immensely thankful to Biswajit Parida, Research Assistant for the project, who gave tremendous support in the study and accompanied me in the various trips made to the field.

Finally I thank my large family for their never-ending love and support.

Seema Mallik

Preface

Globalization has definitely transformed the world and has changed the social, economic and political lives of millions globally. The liberalized and market driven development though irreversible has been responsible for increasing regional disparities around the world. Large sections of society are being excluded from the benefits of this process. Local communities across the globe are resisting resource exploitative and extractive strategies which are not only detrimental to environment but also threaten the lives and livelihood of vulnerable sections of the society. There is a growing insensitivity of the State towards them wherein the marginalized are resisting strategies which are not inclusive and driving them towards further poverty and marginalization. This is becoming a common feature in the Global South.

The impacts of globalization is also visible in India. A booming economy on one side, with poverty and widespread inequalities staring on the other side. India continues to lag behind in Human Development Indicators. It is a paradox. The New Economic Policy (NEP) initiated in the 1990s has definitely catapulted

India to the second fastest growing economy after China. However, there is a growing local resistance to multinational and transnational capital-led investments whose benefits are enjoyed by the rich industrialized nations while depleting and destroying local resources and livlihoods. Many such projects have come not been able to off or have come to a standstill.

Adopting Joel Migdal's state-society approach, this book re-examine the growing conflicts and resistance to present development strategies by local communities in several Third World countries. Migdal's thesis is that state is best understood through its practices, particularly where it reaches out to the society through its policies and institutions. Through accommodations and resistance both have a transformative effect on each other. However, as the present study shows with the increasing practices of a states which fail to accommodate the requirements of society, there is an increasing state-society conflicts. The alignment of neo-liberal states with MNCs and TNCs have created a new capitalist elite who pay scarce attention to needs of the vulnerable in their quest for profits. Land dispossession based on *eminent domain* has become a common feature in the global South.

This conflict is highlighted in this book with focus on India taking the case study of the Odisha. Odisha, despite its mineral wealth and resources continues to be one of the poorest states of India. The state launched heavy industrialization and mining to overcome poverty but many of these projects have been resisted by local communities.

The book therefore argues that these state-centric strategies have failed to accommodate with the local socio-economic needs and are therefore being contested. Rather than building self-reliant societies, new enclosures of dependency are now in the increase. On one hand livelihoods are threatened, and on the other hand government schemes of food and employment are creating greater dependency on the state. Many of these schemes are poorly implemented. Therefore, the book argues that true development will come by building up and strengthening capabilities of local communities through *socially embedded* strategies. This will facilitate in increasing local participation and inclusion and thereby reduce state-society conflicts.

Seema Mallik

Contents

List of Illustrations

Maps

Figures

Tables

1

Development and Contestations: A Perspective

Introduction

India since the 1990s has changed gears from being a 'reluctant pro-capitalist state to a an enthusiastic pro-capitalistic state with a neo-liberal ideology' (Kohli, 2010:499). There is a shift from the Nehru-Mahalanobis model of development through import substitution industrialization (ISI) where development strategies were inward looking towards liberalization of the economy through trade led growth (TLG). This economic transition had become a necessity due to slow growth rates and growing poverty in the country. The Nehruvian mixed-economy approach required an active intervention of the state. The developmental state definitely brought India out of the clutches of colonial economic stagnation and helped in achieving self-sufficiency in food-grain production and industrial growth. However, the economic growth was not sufficient and was criticized as being unbalanced and unsustainable. These social and economic policies adopted by Nehru and successive governments failed to achieve the broad goals which Nehru had envisioned, "the ending of poverty, ignorance and disease and inequality of opportunity" (Dreze and Sen 2002). It failed to provide the minimum basic needs to the population and poverty continued to be widespread. By the 80s the situation became grim and there was as urgent need for reforms. Liberalization was therefore seen as the remedy for the economic ills the country was facing. The 1990s witnessed India discard the state-led growth and embrace the New Economic Policy (NEP) for greater integration with the global market.

THE NEO-LIBERAL FRAMEWORK

The neo-liberal argument is that high growth of gross domestic product (GDP) can be achieved as liberalization of global and domestic markets would create opportunities for the enterprising class in the economy (Hirway, 2012). As a result, the private sectors as well as the external sector (through opening up the economy) push up rate of investment and growth in the economy by attracting capital and new technologies The neo-liberal framework proposes that human well-being can best be advanced by liberating individual entrepreneurial freedoms and skills within an institutional framework characterized by strong property rights, free markets and free trade (Harvey, 2005). These are institutional arrangements considered essential to guarantee individual freedom (*ibid*). Further, the freedom of business and corporations (legally regarded as individuals) to operate within this institutional framework of free market and free trade is regarded as a fundamental good (*ibid*). Private entrepreneurial initiatives are seen as keys to innovation and wealth creation. Thus the neoliberal theory contends poverty can best be eliminated through free markets and free trade. It believes that social good will be maximized by maximizing the frequency of market transactions and it seeks to bring all human actions into the domain of market. Thus globally, since the 1970s there has been an emphatic turn towards neo-liberalism in political-economic practices by almost all states today, either newly emerging states of former Soviet Union or welfare states also. This trend is currently being pursued with full force by the now instruments of globalization that is the International Monetary Fund (IMF), World Bank and World Trade Organization (WTO), and the group of the most industrialized nations in the world the (G8).

However, these agents are being looked at suspicion by the less developed countries who are realising the new imperialistic designs of the advanced countries and their agents. Therefore several critics contend that the rules and regulations of these agents of imperialism are fundamentally unfair to the working of the poor people around the world. Critics believed that the economic, political and cultural integration of the world into a global village is to further subjugate the economies of the Less Developed Countries (LDCs) to the absolute control of the USA and her western allies. David Harvey calls this process of neoliberalization as a "creative destruction" of not only prior institutional frameworks and state sovereignty, but also of divisions of labour, social relations, welfare provisions, attachment to land and ways of life. (Harvey, 2005), Joseph Stiglitz, has argued that the West has seriously mismanaged the process of privatization, liberalization and stabilization and by following its advice several Third World and former Communist states are actually worse off than before (Stiglitz, 2002). The western monopolistic view of creating a universalistic socioeconomic framework for all countries is being increasingly questioned and challenged today. There is a widespread disenchantment with the GDP indices of growth .

Contending views have emerged. Jagdish Bhagawati dismantles the anti-globalization case (Bhagawati, 2004). He persuasively argues that globalization often leads to greater general prosperity in an underdeveloped nation: it can reduce child labor, increase literacy and enhance the economic and social standing of women. Bhagawati in his Hiren Mukharjee Memorial Lecture in 2010 has argued that liberalization has two phases. In the first phase it unleashes the forces of growth, and in the second phase it addresses social inequalities, poverty, health and education with the help of higher revenues generated by the first phase. There is a trickle down of benefits to the underprivileged.

Further, a large number of social scientists whom Pranab Bardhan collectively refers as *anarco-communitarians* have attacked this State-driven developmental strategy (Bardhan, 1987). These economists claim that the neo-liberal strategies despite reducing poverty levels have widened inequalities. There is an increasing urban-rural divide, regional disparities and class conflicts in India. Kohli (2009) has highlighted that the. Economists Dreze' and Sen (2013) have also raised serious questions on India's development programme which has excluded large sections of the society.

Therefore Amartya Sen (Sen, 2000) calls for a broadening of the term 'development' beyond the current narrow focus on economic measures such as per capita

GDP and income levels. He refers to development as the process of real freedom that people enjoy (Sen, 2000). Development should be viewed not in terms of economic measures (e.g. GDP growth, average annual income) but in terms of the real 'freedoms' that people can enjoy such as economic facilities and social opportunities. Sen describes human freedom as both the primary objective and the principle means of development; economic measures are merely the means to this end. Sen frames development as the realization of freedom and the abolishment of 'unfreedoms' such as poverty, famine, starvation, undernourishment, tyranny, poor economic opportunities, systematic social deprivation, neglect of public facilities, intolerance, and over-activity of repressive states (ibid:3). He argues that there is no direct link between a measure such as a country's GNP growth rate and the real freedoms that its citizens enjoy. For example, countries like South Africa and Brazil have a higher per capita GNP but lower life expectancy when compared to Sri Lanka and China (ibid:6). Though recognizing the importance of economic benchmarks, Sen argues for the need for an expanded definition of development to include real human 'freedoms' such as political freedoms, economic facilities, social opportunities, transparency guarantees and protective security (ibid:13-34). The main purpose of development is to spread freedom and its "thousand charms" to the unfree citizens (ibid:). Freedom, Sen persuasively argues, is as once the ultimate goal of social and economic arrangements and the most efficient means of realizing general welfare.

However, neo-liberal strategies involving huge investments in natural resources like land and forests have threatened local communities and forest dwellers whose well-being is at risk. These communities are experiencing increasing stress particularly regarding forceful land dispossession for heavy industrialization, mining and special economic zones. These projects demand huge amount of land and resources, much more than what is required These have created new elite enclosures of living leading to the marginalization and exploitation of local communities, mindless displacement and ecological imbalance. Driven from their own homelands and livelihoods and forced to stay in rehabilitation colonies, the self-sufficient communites in many cases, are forced into a dependency on the state for food. Thus, they are denied elementary freedoms and remain imprisoned in one way or another by economic poverty, social deprivation, political tyranny or cultural authoritarianism. Thus a generation of what Sen describes as "unfree citizens" are created whose welfare and well-being is questioned. A self-reliant local economy is killed and people compelled to lead an alien dependent life wherein *new enclosures of dependency* are created.

India and Neoliberalization

India is no exception, adopting neoliberal policies and practices with the hope of improving the well-being of its population. This is the case of India specifically since the 1990s when the new economic policy was developed to revive a sluggish economy. India has definitely emerged as the second fastest growing economy after China. However, while focusing on human freedom, Dreze' and Sen have argued that though India has made rapid economic expansion in specific fields like computer technology and software, information technology, the absolute deprivation in

India is extraordinary high (Dreze and Sen, 2002). As India progresses into the 21st century "the lives of majority of its citizens continues to be blighted by endemic poverty, under nutrition, ill-health, educational deprivation, environmental degradation and wide-ranging social inequalities" (Dreze and Sen, 2002: vi). The neoliberal development strategies in India are heavily driven by market mechanism and profit motive, thus raising the questions of the *ends* of these economic strategies. The basic needs of vulnerable sections of a highly heterogenous and diverse society have remained unfulfilled. Extensive literature and evidences, have brought to light growing disparities in the country over the years (Dreze' and Sen, 1996; 2002; 2011; 2013; Kohli, 2004; 2010; 2012; Bardhan, 2004; Das, 2014). Despite a fairly rapid economic growth, there has been a parallel growth of inequality also raising strong doubts on the "inclusiveness" of these strategies. Therefore, Kohli has drawn an apt comparison of 'old and new India' as described below:

> *"A sluggish economy and organizational deficiencies were major obstacles to helping the poor during the pre-1980s period.In the new context of a buoyant economy, public resources to help the poor are available. Some of these are indeed being devoted to improving the employment, education and health condition of the poor. What remains in doubt, however, is the depth of commitment of India's-pro-business leaders to the poor;some of these strategies are driven by electoral measures..........as in the past, the state's capacity to reach the poor continues to be limited; improving this capacity will remain*

> *a precondition for successful state intervention on behalf of the poor".* (Kohli, 2012:2).

Thus, in the present context, the benefits of liberalization are being highlighted while rising inequalities and the neglect of the poor and vulnerable sections of the society continue to receive little attention. This growth process has definitely benifitted a small capitalist class, creating more billionaires, a growing middle class while disabling the lower sections of the society like the daily wagers, landless labourers, small farmers, small business to name a few. It has produced dispossession, unemployment, under-employment, casualization, informalization, a heightened level of exploitation, insecurity and inequality (Das, 2014). Natural resources like land, forests, minerals are being given off by the state to corporate houses at throw away prices. The impact of this is felt in rural India which is now driving the people against the state. This has become the reason for growing state-society conflicts and increasing violence where the poor and marginalized are raising their voices against the so called "inclusive" strategies which are threatening or driving them away from their homes and livelihoods.

Therefore there is an urgent need for an *'inclusive participatory growth[1]' where the local economy is integrated with the mainstream rather than weakened* wherein the failures of the neo-liberal frame-work can be undone and the excluded can be gradually included in the developmental process.

Conceptual Framework

By adopting a political economy approach within

the state-society framework, the book has examined and analysed the contemporary land accumulation process which lies at the core of India's growth strategies. It argues that as a result of this forceful loss of land and livelihood, there is increasing poverty and inequality in rural India which is the reason behind the state-society conflicts. Based on empirical evidences from Odisha, the eastern state of India, the book highlights the linkages between poverty and violence of local communities.

Within the state-society framework the book has explored state domination and changes in society. Therefore, understanding the state-society approach becomes paramount in analysing these rising conflicts in India. Edward Shils's centre-periphery model (Parsons & Shils, 1951) emphasised on the dynamism and activism of the centre where the periphery remains a passive receipent. The centre consisting of three primary components i.e. values and beliefs, institutions, and elites moulds the periphery. The nature of structures and beliefs at the periphery matters very little to the elites of the centre. The centre integrates the society through a consensual pattern amoung the elites that assimilates the diverse persons, rules and roles into a centre. Thus the element of consensus or affinity is a powerful assumption of Shils as it explains how society is held and changes brought. Shils saw the source of authority and change as inhering in a witch's brew of elites, institutions, and shared values. (Migdal 2004:6). It ignores the conflict that gradually emerge. By the middle of the twentieth the state created more and more rules to govern the details of people's lives. This resulted in increasing state-directed interventions which began to be resisted by other social organizations in the state.

Many scholars have questioned the deep-rooted Western biases where modernity means western and all historical development and evolution is towards modernity. They have questioned whether this approaches can throw light on the radical changes in the Third World countries accurately which were witnessing shifts in the distribution of social control. Thus, the central political and social drama in recent times has been the battle between the state and other social organizations giving rise to state-society conflicts (Migdal, 1988; 2004)

Joel Migdal[2] presents a model for understanding state capabilities in the Third World based on state-society relations. It challenges the western ideas that there are certain universal and singular set of social norms which all members have internalized. This would create solidarity in society . For other parts of the world, especially the newly formed countries in Asia and Africa where such normative solidarity was presumed to be absent, the focus was on the development of an ethic powerful enough to transform divergent (unharmonious) norms and institutions (often seen as traditional and inferior), assuming that modern, Western values would inevitably triumph in the end (Migdal, 2004:5). This model depicts "society as a melange of social organizations rather than a dichotomous structure" as Shils described. (Migdal 2004). The state is seen as one organization amoung many and is guided by the same rules as others, but on a grander scale. Just like social associations, it seeks social control by having the people incorporate its rules into their strategies of survival, or even by monopolizing individual strategies of survival. "State social control involves the successful subordination of people's own inclinations of social behaviour or behaviour sought by other social organizations in favour of the behaviour prescribed by state rulers." (Migdal, 1988: 22).

This is the key point of his model of state-society interaction: the state and social organizations continually compete for social control. The state, by its very nature, lays claim to the authority to regulate all social relations within its borders, thus pitting it against all social organizations that would resist this undertaking. The dominant authority determines who will make the rules pertaining to certain segments of the population. This may lead to a shift in the available strategies of survival for the affected individuals. This finally can result in breakout of conflict over different issues particularly in very diverse and plural society like India. Migdal therefore emphasises this is the case in weblike societies where the state is unable to achieve greater social control.

> *"The high level of group diversity in weblike societies is the reason for the state's inability to achieve greater social control. In weblike societies, although social control is fragmented and heterogeneous, this does not mean that people are not being governed; they most certainly are. The allocation of values, however, is not centralized. Numerous systems of justice operate simultaneously." (Migdal, 1988:32)*

Thus, under these circumstances, a struggle for social control takes place between the state and communities usually unwilling to cede their privileged position by abandoning social control to the state.

Migdal therefore presents that social organizations including the state need to coexist with society symbiotically. Migdal contends that : *i)* the nature of the state cannot be separated from the nature of societies; and *ii)* the emergence of a strong, capable state can occur only with a tremendous concentration of social control (to the state). Social control requires the state to become a real and symbolic aspect of people's daily survival strategies. When the state fails in doing so, state society conflicts grow.

Therefore, development must address the question of equity[3]. Unless equity becomes intrinsic to development goals, and individuals have the freedom to make their choices for their well-being, inequality persists. Thus, despite three decades of rapid growth, India remains one of the poorest countries where millions are deprived of basic living requirements like food, nourishment, shelter, healthcare, education. In India the trickle down effect of the economic gains has been poor resulting in rising inequality and inequity.

Further, building human capabilities and opportunity, requires security of life and property, like land, natural resources and infrastructure. However, when these are threatened, it results in dissatisfaction amoungst the affected people towards institutions of governance, wherein the state comes in direct conflict with local communities. In India, a neo-liberal state has adopted strategies towards heavy industrialization to generate rapid growth. However, these strategies, which involve huge tracts of forceful land acquisition from farmers, have been met with stiff resistance by local communities across India. These land related conflicts have become central to development in India where several projects have been stalled or not able to take off.

Insights from Odisha

Against this theoretical argument this volume has attempted to grapple with the question of 'development for whom' as the development strategies devised by the state has rarely been able to address the needs of local communities in India and several other countries in the Global South. Huge swathes of population continue a life of poverty and want. Today, there is a lot of debate the world over on how neo-liberal forces are defining the use of resources and also getting the support of the government. The government while supporting theses corporate houses is turning against its own people. Therefore needed the important question is: Development for whom and at what cost? If the people for whom development is claimed are deprived off their land, homes and livelihoods, serious doubts are being raised about this development strategy. This is particulary the case of India, given its diversity and social inequalities.

It is in light, that this volume has explored the state-conflicts in the context of Odisha where the government has launched a massive industrialization programme of about Rs.1,60,000 crore with corporate houses to overcome poverty and infuse growth. The conflicts are against the forceful land acquisition by the government and resistance by communities who are facing increasing threats to their homes and livelihoods.

Odisha is one of the poorest states in India with its gross state domestic product (GSDP) way behind the national GDP. But it is one of the mostly mineral-rich states of the country poised towards rapid industrialization. Recent evidences have shown that economically it has taken off to a high growth phase but as far as poverty is concerned the picture is gloomy. The neo-liberal arguments that economic growth is essential for poverty reduction is being contested. Further, there is an increasing frequency of violence and conflicts between the state and local communities against various industrialization projects and land acquisitions, thus questioning the feasibility of these projects and their claims of addressing social inequalities. Therefore, this volume has drawn insights from the following conflicts in the state

- Posco India at Paradeep (Jagatsinghpur distrcict)
- Vedanta Alumina at Lanjigarh (Kalahandi District)
- Kalinga Nagar (Jajpur Distrct)

It explores the contestation to the neo-liberal policies which, instead of bringing in all sections of society into the growth process are promoting exclusion and marginalization of large section of India's diverse population. Further, there has been a deepening of the democratic institutions and process in India which have strengthened local voices against the state particularly when State-driven economic strategies have become a threat to the lives, customs and livelihood of local communities. While highlighting that economic development is not complete without social and political development, the study reiterates Sen's concept of development, as an expansion of freedom of individuals and opportunities.

Therefore, development from one angle needs to be growth oriented and on the other angle should be sustainable and inclusive in a highly inegalitarian society like India. The same strategies adopted in advanced western countries cannot be juxtaposed on India, ignoring the diversity and plurality. Therfore strategies need to be *'socially embedded'*[4] involving local resources and local people. Although the area of study is Odisha, the volume reflects the debates in the larger domain of the Global South, which is facing similar threats from the western dominated capitalo-centric strategies. This volume will have relevance to policy makers, researchers and students both at the national international levels.

NOTES

1. The United Nations Development Programme (2008) defined inclusive growth as "the process and the outcome where all groups of people have participated in the organization of growth and have benefited equitably from it".
2. Refer Migdal, J.S (1988) *Strong Societies and Weak States: State-Society Relations and State Capabilities in the Thirld –World* (Cambridge University Press) Migdal (2004) *State in Society: Studying how State and Societies Transform and Constitute One Another* (Cambridge University Press)
3. Equity is defined in terms of equal opportunities and avoidance of deprivation in outcome particularly in health and education and consumption levels (WDR Report, 2006).
4. Concept of social embeddedness has been pioneered by Karl Polanyi in his book *The Great Transformation* (1944). His ideas are that 'land, labourand money' are "fictitious commodities" as they are produced for the market. Polanyi explained that they must always remain embedded in the society. Their complete subordination to the market would lead to the economic breakdown and destruction of the society.

2

Development and Conflict in India: Land Grab or Land Rights[1]

2.1 Background

India, since its independence has made significant achievements seen particularly, in the light of India's colonial past. India adopted a democracy which despite several "crisis in governability" (Kohli, 1990:3-32), has survived for over seventy years. Indian democracy has been unique in the sense that it did not adhere to the existing theories that stipulate the preconditions of democracy: India is not an industrialized developed economy; India's businessmen and middle classes do not fully control the country's policies; India was anything but ethnically homogenous and ranked low in a number of attributes of "civic culture" (Kohli, 2001). Today, the achievements of a modern, democratic India are accepted globally.

In the economic front, India's achievements have been enormous, moving from a near-zero growth rate at the time of independence to one of the fastest growing economies in the world today. Table 2.1 presents a summary picture of the growth of the gross domestic product (GDP), from colonial time to the present (Dreze and Sen, 2013; pp-4).

Table 2.1: Growth Rates of India's Gross Domestic Product (GDP) (% per year)

	GDP(%)
Colonial Period	
1900-1 to 1946-47	0.9
Early post-Independent period	
1950-51 to 1960-61	3.7
1960-61 to 1970-71	3.4
1970- 71 to 1980-81	3.4
Recent Decades	
1980-81 to 1990-91	5.2
1990-91 to 2000-01	5.9
2000-01 to 2010-11	7.6

Source: Dreze and Sen (2013) pp-4.

Since the 1990s, India has thrown off pro-socialist development strategies and adopted pro-business strategies under liberalization which has led to rapid economic growth as shown above (Kohli, 2012: 20). However, it is extremely important to note that the societal reach of economic progress in India has been remarkably limited. The revenue generated by rapid economic growth has not been used to expand the social and physical infrastructure in a determined and well-planned way (Dreze and Sen 2013: 8). Further, there is a continued lack of essential social services like schooling, health care, safe drinking water, sanitation to a huge part of the population (Kohli, 2012). While India has been marching forward in terms of GDP growth rate, other countries of South Asia like Bangladesh, Sri Lanka and even Nepal have been overtaking India in terms of social indicators. A much poorer economy like Bangladesh has caught up and overtaken India in terms of important social indicators like life expectancy, immunization of children, infant mortality rate, child undernorishment, maternal mortality and girls' schooling (ibid). Similarly Nepal despite a much lower GDP, has caught up with India. India is now second worst from being the second best in South Asia, twenty years ago. India has been ranked 131 in the 2016 Human Development Index (HDI) among the 188 countries[2]. With a score of 0.624, India has been placed in medium human developed countries.[3]

There is a huge failure in achieving the broad goals which Nehru had envisioned, "the ending of poverty, ignorance and disease and inequality of opportunity", despite a fast growing per capita income (Dreze and Sen, 2002). Therefore, India's development raises the debate over the path of development being taken in a neo-liberal environment. Some argue that a pro-business state has released economic dynamism in India while others argue that this development has benefited a new elite and has been responsible for growing inequality, neglect of the poor, the marginalized, and has led to an increasing state-society conflict. In recent times these conflicts are directed against the state which is acquiring land from small farmers and converting them into industry-infrastructures, threatening the livelihoods of the poor. This development debate will be examined with regard to the resistance of small farmers and other marginalized sections of the society to state policies of forceful land accumulation by the state .

DEVELOPMENT AND LAND ACQUISITION IN INDIA

Land is central to human existence particularly the rural and the urban poor. The World Bank in its report' *'Land policies for Growth and Poverty'* reaffirmed "the need for a careful and differentiated approach as a pre-condition for making a clear policy recommendation in case of land that can help improve both efficiency and equity (World Bank, 2003:xvii). However, given that the historical evolution of property rights is not only a response to economic forces, it is not surprising that the arrangements found in several countries are not optimal either from an economic or a social perspective (ibid).

Land continues to be a fintite source of production, livelihood and security across India. In an highly agrarian economy like India, land performs the crucial role of providing economic security in the absence of alternative employment opportunities and social safety nets (Saha, 2013). While land has always been the single most important asset in rural India, that land is also now increasingly desired by domestic and international capital looking for space to create factories, offices, residential townships, shopping complexes and various forms of infrastructure on a Public Private Partnership (PPP) basis (Levian, 2011:455). The resistance to this accumulation of land by the state has intensified because farmers hardly benefit from economic activity for which their land is desired. So while the state's role in transferring land to private capital has increased with the onset of liberalization, farmer resistance to land dispossession has metamorphosed into a series of small wars across the subcontinent, with SEZs as a prime target (ibid: 455).

Large scale land acquisition for industries, SEZs, IT sectors, real estate have challenged agricultural growth. The small farmers are facing growing threats of loosing their lands to business groups in the name of "development". A "pro-business" (Kohli, 2010) State has become a broker for land acquisition from small farmers mostly scheduled castes and scheduled tribes to provide at throwaway prices to the corporate houses. Therefore, the diversion of land for non-agricultural use like heavy industry, SEZs, urban growth, has been met with resistance by local communities as in Singur in West Bengal, Posco, Vedanta and Kalinganagar in Odisha. Given this situation, the viability of these schemes which make the poor poorer, landless and dependent on the government is questioned. The legal framework of *eminent domain*[4] adopted since colonial period continiues to haunt even today.

Therefore, the question 'development for whom'? Those who are forced dispossession off their lands do not benefit from this business transaction where a new class of those enjoying the profits are created. These areas are highly knowledge-intensive and not labour-intensive which is beyond the capabilities of the vast, poor, illiterate rural farmers of India [Levian (2011)]. Contrary to older forms of dispossession where land was expropriated for the natural resources it could deliver, in SEZs land is dispossessed so that it can be commodified as urban spaces (Levian, 2013a, b; 2011a). Levian gives the case of Mahindra World City in Rajasthan to highlight the functioning of State-corporate nexus (Levian, 2012)[5].

In India, large number of memorandums have been signed for the creation of SEZs on the Chinese model. But unlike China, where SEZs are state-directed, in India it being controlled and manipulated by the private companies to generate maximum profits for themselves. Thus, forceful acquisition of land from the poor farmers by the ruling elite to attract private investors in states has become a part of the ongoing economic reform process in India resulting in increasing state-society conflicts.

These conflicts are most visible in the state of Odisha which is a mineral rich state but is one of the poorest states of India. The state government has signed several MoUs with corporate houses and launched a massive industrialization programme for poverty eradication and generating growth. This is being met with stiff resistance where projects have not been able to take off or have been forced to close down. Most important have been the Posco resistance in Jagatsingpur district, Kalinganagar massacre in Jajpur district where as mentioned earlier, at the outset of 2006, 12 tribals were killed by State forces while protesting specifically against the beginning of construction work by Tata Steel and against wreckless "industrialisation" and forceful eviction; Vedanta Aluminium Limited (VAL) is facing stiff opposition for mining bauxite from Niyamgiri hills at Lanjigarh in Kalahandi acquisition has also raised the question of customary rights, particularly among the landless and tribals who do not possess land records but have drawn their livelihoods and sustenance from it for long. Hence land and land rights remain at the core of a rapidly changing economy like India where agriculture remains the chief livelihood provider to large sections of the population. What is questioned is the way land is acquired by the state in the name of "development", forcing disspossession of land and livelihoods.

This dispossession from land or 'land grab' is now a global phenomenon. Dispossession of land through *eminent domain* was a feature of colonial rule, followed by post colonial states and now neo-liberal economies. Therefore, it becomes important to understand land grab in a neo-liberal economy like India, where the Land Acquisition, Rehabilitation and Resettlement Act, (*LARR Act*, 2013) was enacted followed by *LARR* (Ordinance), 2014 and 2015 to make the process of land acquisition more simpler .This was however, met with countrywide protests and farmers' suicide which forced the Ordinance to be withdrawn on 31st August, 2015.

GLOBAL SOUTH AND "LAND GRAB"

Since the 1980s, there has been a dramatic increase in land acquisition, particularly in the 'global South'. The term 'global South' refers to developing countries which are primarily situated in the southern hemisphere in Africa, Asia and South America. There is a growing evidence accentuating 'land grab' or forceful land acquisition by the state in these areas (Bernstein, 2010;White et al, 2012;Borras Jr et al, 2011; Li, 2010; Banerjee-Guha,2013; Levian, 2013, 2012, 2011).

The phrase 'global land grab' has become a catch-all to describe and analyze the current explosion of large scale (trans)national commercial land transactions (Borras Jr et al, 2011:2010; Wolford,2013; Hall et al, 2011). Around the world, there have been strong reactions from states, corporations, and civil society groups on these large scale land deals. While land grabs are seen as a major threat to the lives and livelihoods of the rural poor, who oppose such commercial land deals others see it as an economic opportunity for the rural poor (Borras et al, 2011). In just one year, from March 2008 to April 2008, an estimated 40 million hectares of land changed hands; the latest World Bank figures suggest that this was twenty times higher than the average annual level of land transfers for the preceding forty years (Arezki et al.,2011:1 in Borras Jr et al, 2011). Economic growth, industrialization and urbanization have been the main reasons behind the conversion of agricultural and forest land for commercial, and infrastructural use.

Harvey (2003) calls it the *'accumulation by dispossession'* (ABD), the new form of imperialism . He uses Marx's concept of "primitive accumulation" which is the process by which non-capitalist social formations are transformed into capitalist ones and workers are separated from the direct access to the means of production leading to their alienation . This is marked by exploitation and accumulation of wealth by the capitalists. Thus capitalism has created a hegemonic ideology of prosperity which has led to a close partnership with the state in neo-liberal thought. Together, they have embarked on "land accumulation" at cheap rates from the small farmers leading to greater levels of poverty and alienation of the poor in underdeveloped areas. However, ABD differs from 'primitive accumulation' in the sense that while *'primitive accumulation'* was understood as a process of coercive appropriation creating the pre-conditions for capitalist accumulation, ABD is now seen as a process that allows global capital to find new outlets in advanced capitalism (Levian, 2012). 'Accumulation by dispossession" opens up fertile terrain for understanding the proliferation of contemporary land grabs in India (Li,2009; Levian, 2013, 2012, 2011;Menon and Nigam 2007; Banerjee-Guha 2008, 2010;Sampat 2008; Sarkar, 2007) and the changing role of the State.

However, Levian argues that the existing theoretical perspectives, whether Marx's primitive accumulation or Harvey's *accumulation by dispossession*, are not adequate for understanding the political economy of land dispossession under capitalism-in India or elsewhere (Levian 2015:146). This is because both theories underplay the role of the state. Therefore, Levian advances the concept of *"regimes of dispossession"* as a better way of understanding how dispossession is politically organized in different socio-historical contexts to serve different class interests (Levian, 2013). Thus, *"regimes of dispossession'* are forms of coercive redistribution that states use to facilitate different forms of accumulation and class interests in different periods. It emphasises that while dispossession is an ongoing process of capitalism and changes under different historical forms of capital formation, it is ultimately a political process, mediated by the state and thus can be stopped by non-compliance of rural people. Tanya Li (2009; 2007) highlights this aspect in her analysis of large parts of rural Asia, in India and Indonesia and assigns two reasons for growing poverty. Firstly, the new round of enclosures have dispossessed large numbers of rural people from their land and secondly the low absorption of their labour, which is "surplus" to the requirements of capital accumulation (Li, 2009:67). She further adds that no one has the market incentive to keep these 700 million poor Asians who live on less than a dollar a day, alive from day to day or generation to next.

As mentioned earlier, in India, there is a gradual decline of the contribution of agriculture to the GDP compared to industry and services. The focus of reforms is on non-agricultural economy which is responsible for the increasing pauperization of the rural poor particularly leading to greater inequality in the society. There is a growing consensus amoung all parties that agriculture is less profitable and needs to be replaced by industries. Therefore, dispossession of land from small and medium farmers to build industries under the 'veil of public purpose' has created unjust growth patterns in India. The justification put forward by the state/companies that this will create job opportunities is nothing but a myth. The ground reality is that these poor farmers are ill-suited for any jobs in these highly knowledge intensive zones. Therefore, rather than grabbing land to create 'employment opportunities' to improve the lives of the poor, there is an urgent need to enhance their freedom of choice and opportunities to help themselves rather than making them more dependent on the state. The current populist measure of the state government of providing one rupee per kg rice is an example in this direction which has damaged rural economy further. Evidences from the field have indicated that there is a decline in cultivation as people are getting rice cheaply under the public distribution system and then selling it at a higher price. Fields are lying barren in many parts of the state which depends on food supplies from its neighbours particularly West Bengal and Andhra Pradesh.

Therefore in a state like Odisha, both industry and agriculture need to balance each other. When agriculture is being sidelined for industry, there is bound to be increasing poverty related to land and food security. Secondly, there is a need for enhanced dimensions of human development like health, education, infant mortality rates, life expectancy etc as essential features of growth. Industrial growth has to be integrated with human development.

NOTES

1. Earlier version of this chapter titled Land Grab or Land Rights: understanding Land Acquisition in India', **appeared in the** The Indian Journal of Political Science, Vol LXXVII, No. 2, April-June, 2016, pp. 217-222. ISSN No.2277-8160,
2. HDI is a measure for assessing countries progress in three basic dimensions of human development: a long and healthy life (life expectancy), access to knowledge and access to a decent standard of living. Countries are ranked based on scale ranging between 0 (low) to 1 (high).
3. Top three countries: Norway (0.949 score), Australia (0.939) and Switzerland (0.939). SAARC countries: Sri Lanka (73) and Maldives (105) were placed in "high human development" category, followed by India (131), Bhutan (132), Bangladesh (139), Nepal (144), Pakistan (147) and Afghanistan (169). BRICS Countries: India ranks lowest among BRICS nations. Russia (49), Brazil (79), China (90), South Africa (119) and India (131). (UNDP, 2016)
4. Eminent domain : The doctrine of eminent domain refers to the power to take private property for public use by a state, municipality, or private person or corporation authorized to exercise functions of public character, following the payment of just compensation to the owner of that property.
5. Mahindra World City in Rajasthan, is a multipurpose 'integrated industrial city', 25 km from Jaipur, which is supposed to include the largest IT-SEZ in India. The Rajasthan government acquired 3000 acres of land in nine villages of which 2000 acres were privately owned and 1000 acres was government land. This was handed over to the $ 7 billion Mahindra and Mahindra Company to create a SEZ. (Levian 2012:946).

3

Land Rights in India with Special Reference to Odisha[1]

Large scale land acquisition for industries, special economic zones (SEZs), IT sectors, real estate have not only challenged the agricultural growth, but pose a threat to the poor, who face the dangers of loosing their lands and their livelihoods ,in the name of "development". There are studies recognizing that the changes brought about by neo-liberal global policies have also resulted in the growing self assertion of communities facing the brunt of the market-driven development process (Shah, 2002). Debates on development in developing countries have, however, paid less attention to these conflicts related to struggles of the people affected by the larger development strategies of the state, and the situation in India in this regard is no different. Land acquisition by the state for various "development programmes" has in fact become the bone of contention between local communities and the state ,particularly where these communities derive their livelihoods from the land being acquired. Therefore, the viability of these schemes which make the people landless and dependent on the government or industrial houses is being doubted. Therefore, the question arises whether this growth is benefiting all sections of the society or is it encouraging disparities in the society? Is it the right direction the country is moving towards?

There is, therefore, an urgent need to reexamine land rights to understand the processes of land acquisition set in motion by the neo-liberal policies giving rise to conflicts between State and local communities. This chapter examines land rights and ownership in the state of Odisha, with a focus on the Scheduled Tribes.

This chapter will first, trace the history of some important land reforms in India, as examining all land acts is beyond the scope of this paper. This will be followed by land reforms particularly concerning tribals in Odisha. A comprehensive analysis of the Forest Rights Act (2006) will be made thereafter followed by the concluding remarks

3.1 Historical Background of Land Rights in India

Land for generations has been regarded both as an economic and also a social commodity. The land distribution in India is skewed. Two percent of landholders own 25 percent of the land whereas 98 percent of the landholders own just 75 percent of the land (Census 2001). Around 43 percent of rural households in the country are landless. Poverty in India, is linked to the absence of land rights to a vast majority of rural and tribal population. The Scheduled Caste (SC) and Scheduled tribes (ST)are however most disadvantaged as far as possession of land is concerned. According to the 2001 Census 64 percent of SC and 36 percent of ST are agricultural labourers compared to 31% of the rest (Census 2001). This has resulted in high poverty levels among scheduled groups. This has made them more vulnerable to social injustice and exploitation. Therefore, land reforms have been central to bring about an egalitarian society and check the exploitation of vulnerable groups. Several laws have been passed before and after independence but they have failed to check land alienation of both tribals and non-tribals by the state. Forceful land acquisition has increased under the state-corporate nexus, where powerful business interests are directing state policies.

Forceful land acquisition in India can be traced to British colonialism. The British adopted an exploitative land and revenue policy and forcefully acquired land on a large scale particularly in tribal areas. They established the Zamindari system which helped the upper caste elites to consolidate their positions. The British policy in India was based on the *doctrine of eminent domain* which was influenced by the e*nclosure movement* in England in the 18th century. The doctrine of *eminent domain* refers to the power to take private property for public use by a state, municipality, or private person or corporation authorized to exercise functions of public character, following the payment of just compensation to the owner of that property. It originated in Europe in 1625 in the works of Hugo Grotius and Samuel Pufendorf where Grotius argued that the property of subjects lay under the eminent domain of the state that may use, alienate and even destroy the property in the case of extreme necessity and for public utility (Sampat,2013). David Harvey (2003; 2005)) calls it *'accumulation by dispossession'* (ABD), the new form of imperialism . He uses Marx's concept of "primitive accumulation" which is the process by which non-capitalist social formations are transformed into capitalist ones and workers are separated from the direct access to the means of production leading to their alienation This is marked by exploitation and accumulation of wealth by the capitalists. Thus capitalism has created a hegemonic ideology of prosperity which has led to a close corporate partnership with the state in neo-liberal thought. Together, they embarked on "land accumulation" at cheap rates from the small farmers leading to greater levels of poverty and alienation of the poor in underdeveloped areas.

In India, this doctrine was reflected in the Indian Constitution through laws which facilitated the state to acquire land forcibly. The British passed *the Land Reforms and Land Acquisition Act (LAA) 1894* which saw the application of doctrine of *eminent domain*. The British and the land-owning elites consolidated their positions while "depeasantising" the tribals and lower caste peasants (Mohanty, 2001). This led to resentment and tribal rebellions across the country[2]. Thus, land reforms became crucial for national planning and attainment of socio-economic emancipation of the deprived groups.

Therefore, immediately after independence, land reform laws were enacted from the 1950s to break the concentration of land with the zamindars and to strengthen the rights of the landless. As land is a state subject, this led a large number of legislative measures for the protection of the deprived groups by individual states. These legislations imposed ceilings on large holdings and attempted to redistribute land amoung the landless. However, the land reforms to attain redistributive justice and check land alienation of the tribals, was opposed by the landed elite for vested interests and they used their power to manipulate records. It was found that many big farmers produced false medical certificates to establish the incapacity of tribals to cultivate their lands and managed to get these lands on lease for fixed periods, after which land is seldom returned to the tribals (Murdia, 1975 in Mohanty, 2001:386). Thus tribals due to their illiteracy and ignorance of land reforms were duped by the non-tribals and their alienation continued. As the fervor for land reforms died down, the "development" projects of the state took shape and by 2002, resulted in the displacement of 60 million people (of which the majority have been tribals (Fernandes, 2008). This is because tribal dominated areas are also mineral rich areas, where mining and industrialization have not only displaced them but have also threatened their livelihoods. The claims that industrialization is the means to remove the poverty and bring about growth stands challenged as these regions are the most backward areas in the country. Odisha, Chattisgarh, Jharkand, Bihar ,Madhya Pradesh, despite their mineral wealth are the poorest states in the country (GOI, 2011).

The Supreme Court of India from 1950-1970 adopted several protective measures for the weaker sections of the society including the tribals. The Fifth Schedule of the Constitution contains provisions as to the administration and control of Scheduled Areas and Scheduled Tribes in the States other than Assam, Meghalaya, and Mizoram[3]. The Sixth Schedule contains provisions of administration of tribal areas in these states. According to Article 342(1) of the Constitution, the President of India, may with respect to any state or Union Territory and where it is a state, in consultation with the governor thereof by public notification specify the tribes or tribal communities which shall for the purpose of the constitution be deemed to be Scheduled Tribe.

Supreme Court however in the early phase struck down several land legislations on the ground that they violated the right to property which was a fundamental right under Article 19(1) of the Constitution. This led to protests from Parliament and as a result land reform laws related were moved to Ninth Schedule by the First Constitutional Amendment, where they were beyond judicial review. Finally, right to property was removed from being a fundamental right by the 44th Constitutional Amendment Act, 1978. This strengthened the power of eminent domain of the state. The colonial statue *Land Acquisition Act, 1894* continued will slight amendments, providing for compulsory acquisition of land for *"public purpose"*. The *Coal Bearing Areas (Acquisition and Development) Act (CBAA), 1957* was enacted specially for coal mining. This directly and drastically affected the tribal population as most of the coal reserves are located in forest areas inhabited by tribals.

The *CBAA, 1957* along with *LAA, 1894* empowered the central government to acquire mining rights with ease thus displacing and threatening the livelihood of the tribals. Thus the existing land reforms have encouraged more inequalities and conflicts in society while overstretching the power of the state over economically, socially and politically marginalized population. Under both these Acts the government can acquire land for "public purpose". The latest version, *The Right to Fair Compensation and Transparancy in Land Acquisition, Rehabilitation and Resettlement (RTFCT-LARR) Act, 2013*, elaborates in details this expanded scope of land acquisition and state's power of eminent domain. It attempts to rectify the archaic *LAA, 1894* and makes the legal entitlements to compensation and rehabilitation and resettlement. But it continues to elaborate on the "public purposes" clause. This opens up new doors for the state to favour private companies and also multinational corporations to acquire land cheaply at the expense of poor farmers and forest dwellers. The misuse of the de-notification clause protects the lands of rich farmers who are hand-in-hand with the state officials .

However despite its many shortcomings it was a significant step towards protecting tribal rights. The FRA, 2006 has been another landmark Act which attempts to undo the injustices to the tribals and other forest dwellers.

THE PANCHAYATS (EXTENSION TO SCHEDULE AREAS) ACT, 1996 (Also called PESA or Tribal Self-Rule Law)

This Act provides for the extension of Panchayati Raj Institutions[4] to Scheduled Areas. It has empowered Gram Panchayats[5] with wide-ranging powers and functions. In the context of natural resources, PESA specifically grants the Gram Sabha control over minor minerals, planning and management of water bodies, management of minor forest produce, and alienation of land (including the power to restore any alienated land of a Scheduled Tribe). As far as forests are concerned, PESA endows special powers to the Gram Sabha, regarding the ownership of minor forests produce (MFP), as these are vital components of tribal economy and sustenance. Most Schedule V[6] states including Odisha have enacted their state Acts under PESA. Schedule Areas, are those areas of tribal concentration that have been declared by the Presidential Order on Scheduled Area under Article 244 of the Indian Constitution[7]. These include the states of Andhra Pradesh, Madhya Pradesh, Chhattisgarh, Jharkhand, Odisha, Gujarat, Rajasthan, Maharashtra and Himachal Pradesh. This significant legislation was expected to have far reaching consequences in the social, economic and cultural life of tribal people in Scheduled Areas, and increase their control over their local natural resources. According to this Act, every Gram Sabha (consisting of all adult voters of a self-defined community) is empowered to "safeguard and preserve the traditions and custom of the people, their cultural identity, community resources and the customary mode of dispute resolution" (GOI,1996, Clause 4d). The Act also assigns the Gram Sabha 'to approve the plans , programmes and projects for social and economic development before such plans, programmes, projects are taken up for implementation by the Panchayat at the village level,' (Clause 4e).

PESA makes it mandatory to seek the permission of Gram Sabha before acquisition of land in Scheduled Areas for development projects and before re-settling or re-habilitating persons affected by these projects. It also empowers the GP to prevent alienation of land in Scheduled areas and to take appropriate steps to restore any unlawfully alienated land of a Scheduled Tribe. However, in spite of being one of the most empowering legislations regarding tribal administration in India, it is marred by several ambiguities. Most of the provisions are subservient to the Joint Forest Management (JFM) rules.

In June 1990, the Ministry of Environment and Forests (MOEF) issued a circular providing for the '*Involvement of Village Communities and Voluntary Agencies in the Regeneration of Degraded Forests*' (GoI, 1990). This paved the way for the adoption of Joint Forest Management (JFM) resolution. This is an attempt to legally forge a partnership between Forest Department (FD) and the local community where the latter are expected to share in both responsibilities as well as the benefits that would be generated (Ghate, 2003). Thus JFM, which begun as an experiment to involve communities in forest protection, has now become a major national program. This dramatic shift in the approach of government towards forest dwelling communities is an attempt to assimilate the interests of different groups within the communities.

However, JFM guidelines do not even mention PESA indicating the low importance given by Ministry of Environment Forests (MOEF) to its provisions and their potential bearing on the JFM framework in Schedule V areas. While PESA mandates community based forest management by Gram Sabhas, JFM establishes new village communities under the supervision of the Forest Department. Further, "PESA co-exists with totally contrary legislation such as the Land Acquisition, Wild Life Protection, Forest Conservation and the Indian Forest (1927) Acts with no clarity about which is to prevail over the others" (Sarin,Sundar *et al.*, 2003:6). The lack of central government commitment to tribal empowerment is evident from the fact that while PESA remains unimplemented it has proposed the amending of Schedule V of the Constitution itself to open up tribal areas for commercial exploitation by national and multinational corporate interests (Pattanaik, 2001). In short, all the provisions of PESA related to natural resource governance are rendered ineffective on the ground due to the foot-dragging or inattention on the part of the government itself.

Further, despite the enactments of the PESA, all matters concerning land acquisition and leasing of land for mineral purposes are decided in accordance with the LAA, 1894 and Coal Bearing Areas (Acquisition and Development) Act of 1957 and the Gram Sabha is sidelined. On one hand the relevant laws and procedures that could have made land acquisition stringent are being slowly diluted. On the other hand, the operations for land acquisition do not follow what has been agreed upon. PESA has been recognized as 'progressive', but its implementation has been poor and it has been violated at various levels by different states in India. This is because panchayat is a state subject, and states with Schedule V areas had to make changes in their respective panchayat acts in accordance to the central PESA Act. In most states there has been a partial implementation and rules were formulated with major provision of PESA being eliminated. The provisions particularly relating to powers of gram panchayats to land acquisition in many states has been violated. Land continues to be acquired from tribals by force and fraud. However, PESA generated great political awareness among the tribals so much so that the government passed the *The Scheduled Tribes and Other Traditional Forest Dwellers (Recognition of Forest Rights) Act, 2006 or the Forest Rights Act (FRA), 2006*. It was on the strength of this Act that the *Dongria kondhas,* a particularly vulnerable tribal group in Odisha, prevented UK based multi-national company Vedanta from mining bauxite from the *Niyamgiri hills,* which is sacred to the tribals.

THE SCHEDULED TRIBES AND OTHER TRADITIONAL DWELLERS (RECOGNITION OF FORESTS RIGHTS ACT, (FRA) 2006

In a significant admission by on June 21st 2004 before the Supreme Court, the Government of India stated that the "historic injustice done to the tribal forest dwellers through non-recognition of their traditional rights must be finally rectified". This was a historic departure of the colonial practice of "eminent domain", adopted by independent India, where forests were regarded as property of the state; to be exploited at will without consideration for local indigenous human populations. The earlier legislations like the Indian Forest Act, 1927; the Wildlife Protection Act, 1972; and the Forest Conservation Act, 1980, were based on the principle that the state is the guardian of the forests while tribals and forest dwellers were the destroyers of forests. These ignore the fact that tribals were the natural guardians of the forests as their livelihood and very existence depended on forests. This conflict resulted in a long drawn battle between the State and forest communities. There was an unprecedented mobilization of forest communities for rights over their land and forests on which they were traditionally dependent.

The Scheduled Tribes and Other Traditional Forest Dwellers (Recognition of Forest Rights) Act, 2006, hereafter FRA was enacted as a result of this growing voices of dissent of forest dwellers. This Act is crucial to the rights of millions of tribals and other forest dwellers across the country as it provides for the restitution of deprived forest rights, including both individual rights to cultivated lands in forestland and community rights over common property resources (FRA, 2006). This Act "recognizes and vests forest rights and occupation in forestland in forest dwelling Scheduled Tribes and other traditional forest dwellers who have been residing in such forests for generations but whose rights could not be recorded; to provide a framework for recording the forest rights so vested and the nature of evidence required for such recognition and vesting in respect of forest land"[8]. The Act confers forest rights to Scheduled Tribes in occupation of forest land prior to 13th December 2005 and to other traditional forest dwellers who have been in occupation of forest land, up to a maximum of four hectares, for at least three generations, i.e. 75 years., These rights are heritable but not alienable or transferable. Forest rights include among other things, the right to hold land and live on it under individual or common occupation for habitation, self-cultivation for livelihood and so on. It further confers "forest rights on ancestral lands and their habitats which were not recognized during the colonial period as well as independent India resulting in historical injustice to the forest dwelling Scheduled Tribes and other traditional forest dwellers who are integral to the very survival and sustainability of the forest ecosystems" (FRA, 2006). For the first time the FRA, 2006, address the long standing insecurity of tenurial and access rights of forest dwelling Scheduled Tribes and other traditional forest dwellers including those who were forced to relocate their dwelling due to State development. It empowers the Gram Sabha (*Palli Sabha*) as the competent authority to initiate the process of determining the nature and extent of forest rights of individuals or the community The FRA recognises 14 types of pre-existing rights of forest dwellers on all cetegories of forestland, including protected areas. The most significant rights include (FRA, 2006):

i. Individual rights over cultivation and homesteds in forestlands, that is individual forest rights (IFR)

ii. Community forest rights for use and access to forestland and resources (CFR). These include rights to firewood, grazing and other produce for subsistence; rights over minor forest produce; waterbodies and fishes; rights to access biodiversity; intellectual property and traditional knowledge, etc.

iii. Community forest resource (CFR) rights to use, manage and govern forests within the traditional boundaries of the villages;

iv. The empowerment of right-holdersand/or gram sabhas for conservation and protection of forests, wildlife, biodiversity, and their natural and cultural heritage.

Thus the FRA has the potential to advance the goals of inclusive sustainable development, bringing millions of forest dwellers into the mainstream, by giving them their basic right to life and dignity.

The result of this landmark legislation has been the rejection of Vedanta Aluminium and Orissa Mining Corporation's plan for bauxite mining in Niyamgiri hills by 12 gram sabhas of Rayagada and Kalahandi districts of Odisha by the indigenous *Dongria Kondh* tribe (discussed later).

Another landmark legislation which has attempted to undo the archaic LAA, 1894, was the *The Right to Fair Compensation and Transparency in Land Acquisition, Rehabilitation and Resettlement (RTFCT-LARR) Act, 2013.* However, despite tall claims of being pro-farmers it continues to facilitate the State in forceful acquisition of land from farmers.

3.4 THE RIGHT TO FAIR COMPENSATION AND TRANSPARANCY IN LAND ACQUISITION, REHABILITATION AND RESETTLEMENT ACT, (RTFCT-LARR) 2013

The Right to Fair Compensation and Transparency in Land Acquisition, Rehabilitation and Resettlement (RTFCT-LARR) Act, was passed in 2013. The euphoria generated at the time gave the impression that the injustices of archaic LAA, 1894 was finally undone. This was a pro-farmer legislation with noble intentions of making the legal entitlements to compensation, rehabilitation and resettlement. It attempts to rectify the archaic *LAA, 1894* but it continues to elaborate on the "public purposes" clause. The Act has expanded the scope of "public purpose" to include the scope of private sector also. It has drawn a final long list of undertakings, also including some non-public or private activities.

Thus the Land Act, 2013, elaborates in details the expanded scope of land acquisition and state's power of eminent domain. The land acquired by the state can be allocated to private companies under this act. As a result, rather than safeguarding the rights and interests of vulnerable sections of society, the Act has made land acquisition easier by expanding the scope of "public purpose". The concept of "public purpose", under neo-liberal strategies are shaped by the profit-motive of private investors, particularly the multi-national corporations. This has increased inequalities and wealth gaps between the rich and the poor in the country.

The Act required that 80% of affected landowners give approval to land acquisition for private projects and 70% approval for public private partnerships (PPP) projects. This provision has however been exempted from applying to five types of projects in the 2014 Ordinance and the *The Right to Fair Compensation and Transparency in Land Acquisition, Rehabilitation and Resettlement (RTFCT-LARR)(Amendment) Bill, 2015*. This seeks to amend *LARR* Act, 2013. The Bill creates five special categories of land use: 1. defence 2. rural infrastructure 3. affordable housing 4. industrial corridors set-up by the appropriate Government and its undertakings (in which case the land shall be acquired up to one kilometre on both sides of designated railway line or roads for such industrial corridor), 5. infrastructure projects including PPP projects (LARR, Bill 2015). The Bill exempts the above five categories from the LARR Act, 2013, which required the consent of 80% of land oweners incase of private projects and 70% consent of land owerners in case of public private partnership projects. Further the Bill also exempts these five categories from the requirements of Social Impact Assessment (SIA), imposed by LARR, 2013, to identify those affected by land acquisition. The Bill changes acquisition oflandfor private companies mentioned in LARR Act, 2013 to acquisition for "private entities" (LARR, Bill, 2015). A private entity may include companies and non-profit organizations. Further, according to LARR Act, 2013 land will be returned to the original ownerif it is unused for five years. However, LARR, Bill 2015 scraps the "five years" limit at present to "a period specified for setting up of any project or for five years whichever is later".

This opens up new doors for the state to favour private companies and also multinational corporations to acquire land cheaply at the expense of poor farmers. Thus while obtaining consent from farmers was the rationale of the Act, in reality it has hardly paid attention to the genuine needs of farmers. This has become the main casualty in the Ordinance which has eliminated the need to acquire consent of farmers in five types of projects. Secondly the compensation and rehabilitation provisions have become more and more diluted. Despite early suggestions of fixing compensations at six times the government fixed values, the final bill finally reduced this to four times the rate in rural areas and two times in urban areas.

The countrywide protests against Land Acquisition (Amendment) Ordinance (2014) and LARR, Bill 2015, has created the impression that the goodness of 2013 is being washed down. However, none are pro-farmer but both are mechanisms to dispose farmers, particularly small farmers off their land, through material compensation in a neo-liberal state. The objective is to work out a compromise to end land wars across the country. As reported in the *Times of India* (March 31, 2015), an estimated projects valued at Rs 6 lakh crore is stalled due to land acquisition issues. A study by the Society for the Promotion of Wasteland Development (SPWD) and Rights and Resources Initiative (RRI) has highlighted that a quarter of India's districts are witnessing mass protests over land acquisition issues. It has identified 252 land conflicts spread over 165 districts spanning over spanning over 165 districts in practically all states. This is an increase of over 40% over 2012 when an earlier study had recorded 177 disputes in 130 districts (TOI, March 31, 2015). Thus the LARR (2013) and LARR (Amendment) Ordinance 2014 and 2015 have little to offer to farmers except land values.

Further, as the Act stands today, any land acquisition and compensation process is a bureaucratic nightmare which only benefits those who occupy the seats of power. This is because from the time of social impact assessesment (SIA) to the time of payment of compensation and acquisition of land, different levels of bureaucracy and assessment committees are involved which are centres of confusion and hassle to the farmers. The farmers face double disaster of loosing land and not receiving necessary compensation in time. Here I would like to mention that farmers displaced for the Hirakud Dam in Odisha in 1957 have not yet received compensation for their lands. This is just one example amongst many in the country. It is always the small farmers who are most badly hit by this forced acquisition. Therefore, projects across the country are being met with stiff resistance and farmers presently are rejecting compensation. Posco the Korean company signed a MoU with the State government in 2005, but has not been able to start till date because of local resistance. Posco had initially asked for 4004 acres of land, but scaled down its demands to 2753 acres. Agitation continued and the company has finally decided to pull off and "freeze" its $12million project in the state (*TOI,* 17 July, 2015) (details in the following chapter).

3.5 ODISHA: A BACKGROUND

Odisha[9], situated on the eastern coast, has a landmass of I,55,707sq km and a population of 3.68crore as per 2001 Census is divided into 30 districts.It is one of the twenty-ninth states of India and is located on the eastern coast of the country (Refer map, Fig:3.1)). It is surrounded by the states of West Bengal to the north-east, Jharkhand to the north, Chattisgarh to the west and north-west, and Andhra Pradesh to the south. Odisha has 485 kilometres (301 miles) of coastline along the Bay of Bengal on its east. It is the ninth largest state by area, and the eleventh largest by population. It is also the 3rd most populous state of India in terms of tribal population. The Scheduled Area[10] of the State accounts to 44.7% of the State's geographical area (Economic Survey, GoO, 2011-12). The tribal population mostly inhabit the western hilly and southern regions of the state, in close proximity to forests in the districts of Koraput, Sundargarh, Mayurbhanj, Rayagada, Kalahandi and Bolangir (Odisha Development Report, GOI, 2002). These districts are amoung the most poorest regions of the state. As per 2001 Census, the Scheduled Tribe (ST) population of the State is 8,145,081. This constitutes 22.1 percent of the total population of the

State and 9.7 per cent of the total tribal population of the country. The state holds 3rd and 11th rank among the States/UTs in terms of ST population and the proportion of ST population to total population of the State respectively. The State has a total of sixty two (62) Scheduled Tribes, and all have been enumerated in the 2001 census. The Scheduled Tribe population in the State is overwhelmingly rural, with 94.5 per cent residing in villages. District wise distribution of ST population shows that Malkangiri has the highest proportion of STs (57.4 per cent) followed by Mayurbhanj (56.6 per cent), Rayagada (55.8 per cent) and Nabarangapur (55 per cent). Puri district has the lowest by proportion of STs (0.3 per cent).

The Scheduled Caste (SC) population of the Odisha, as per 2001 census is 6,082,063. This constitute 16.5 percent of the total population of the State. The State holds eleventh rank among all the States in terms of the scheduled caste population (Census 2001). The scheduled castes are predominantly rural with 88.4 per cent residing in villages. Among the districts, the scheduled caste have the highest concentration in Sonepur district with a share of 23.6 per cent to the total population, followed by Jajapur (23 per cent) and Boudh (21.9 per cent) districts. Gajapati district has the lowest proportion of the scheduled caste population (7.5 per cent). Both SCs and STs constitute a large population of landless and marginal farmers (UNDP, 2008).

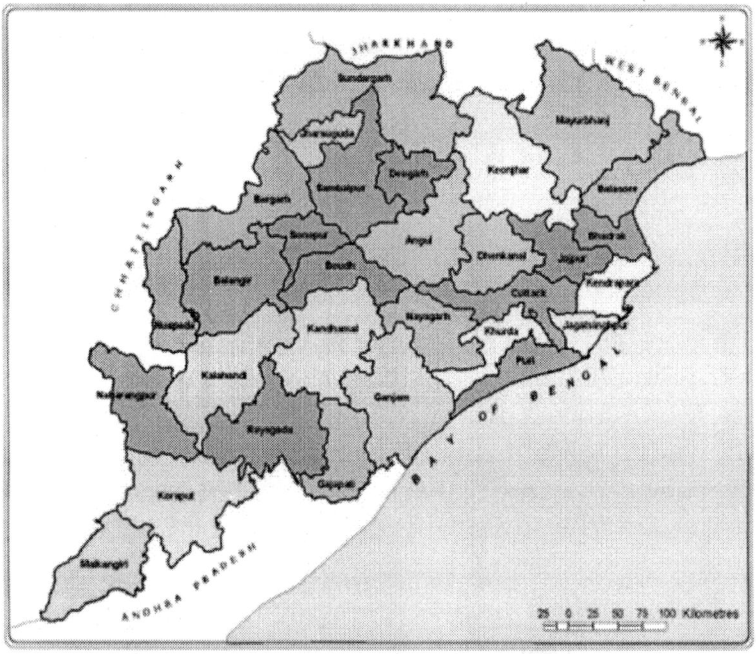

Map of Odisha : Fig 3.1

Source: www.mapsofodisha.nic.in

Odisha as mentioned earlier, is one of the poorest states in India with huge mineral deposits of coal, iron ore, bauxite to name a few. Odisha reflects the Indian growth-development dichotomy. It has been showing a steady 8% to 9% growth rate (Economic Survey of Odisha, 2011-12). At the same time it has one of the lowest human development indices in the country. In recent years, the Government of Odisha has signed numerous accords for private investment in the mining and industrial sector to overcome poverty and backwardness of the state. However, this is expected to cause massive deforestation in the ecologically fragile coastal areas and drought prone western and southwestern Odisha, and resultant loss of farm land and forest land, affecting both livelihood and food security of a vast population comprising of mainly marginal farmers and tribal groups (UNDP, 2009).

3.6 LAND REFORMS IN ODISHA

The state of Odisha was carved out of Madras Presidency and Central Province of Bengal and Bihar in 1936. As a result, a skewed land revenue system existed. There were no uniform land rights across the state .Different revenue systems and tenancy laws existed throughout Odisha. For example the two most common systems of revenue assessment prevalent then were – *Zamindari* and *Ryotwari*[11]. The *Zamindari* system existed in districts like Cuttack, Puri, Balasore and Angul, whereas the *Ryotwari system existed* in parts of Sambalpur district . In addition, there were 24 princely states, which were controlled by the British through a subsidiary alliance, (UNDP, 2008). As a result revenue and tenancy laws in the State varied. The Bengal revenue system was implemented in districts like Balasore, Cuttack and Puri (vide The Bengal Rent Act, 1859) and was replaced by The Bengal Tenancy Act, 1885 and then The Orissa Tenancy Act which was introduced in 1913. The Madras revenue system was exercised in Koraput, Ganjam and parts of Phulbani districts as per the Madras Estate Land Act, 1908. The system applied for both the *Zamindari* and *Ryotwari* areas; in the latter, the rights of the landholders were governed by executive instructions, whereas in the former, landholders could freely sublet land to tenants who however, enjoyed no protection under the law. The Central Province revenue system (vide Central Province Land Revenue Act 1881/1917 and Tenancy Act, 1898/1920) was prevalent in Sambalpur and Nuapada districts. The princely states had separate land settlements and revenue regulations under the Government of India Act, 1935.

The Government of Odisha realized that access to and control over land resources hold the key to poverty alleviation and land reforms is a prerequisite to development. Therefore, it has been one of the first states to implement land reforms by formulating progressive land laws. While in most states, measures taken to check land alienation of tribals and lower caste have not been clearly defined, in Odisha several tenancy regulations have been framed from time to time, with the objective to bring about uniformity in the various existing laws. Some of the important reforms that were implemented were: *the Orissa Tenancy Act,(Amendment of 1946); Orissa Tenancy (Amendment) Act, 1947; the Orissa command Forests and Private Lands Act, 1948*. The two most significant legislations as far as the Scheduled Tribes were concerned were the implementation of the *Orissa Scheduled Areas Transfer of Immovable Property (by Scheduled Tribes), Regulation, 2 of 1956* (OSATIP) Act and the Orissa *Land Reform (O.L.R) Act 1960*. The OSATIP, 1956 and the OLR Act, 1960 are the present statutes governing transfer of tribal land i.e. land settled in the name of the tribals. The former prohibits transfer of lands from members of STs to non-STs. It also regulates the transfer the transfer of private land from scheduled tribes and castes to non-scheduled groups, in Scheduled areas of Odisha. Section 3(1) of this law originally stated that any transfer of property by a member of a scheduled tribe shall be null and void unless it is made to another member of a scheduled tribe or with the prior consent of the competent authority. It provided for restoration of land transferred illegally from tribals to non-tribals (Section 3(2)) and provided for a penalty of up to Rs. 200/- acre of land for each year the property was held (Section 7(1)). The above law was amended by regulation I of 1997, wherein a clause had been inserted that no Scheduled Tribe shall be allowed to transfer land if after such a transfer the total land owned by ST will be reduced to less than one standard acre[12] (as defined in Orissa Land Reforms Act, 1960). The amendment also increased the maximum fine amount from Rs. 200/- per acre per year to Rs. 2000/- per acre per year.

However, alienation of tribal land continued and the government amended the Regulation once again by Regulation 2 of 2002 and has made the act much more stringent. The salient features of the amended laws are: (Regulation 2, OLR, 1960)

- Section (3) of the law states that any transfer of property by a member of a Scheduled Tribe in Scheduled Areas to a non-tribal is not permitted.
- No tribal owner can transfer land to even another ST if the total land remaining with the Tribal is less than two acres of irrigated land or five acres of unirrigated land.
- All transfers from ST to non-STs between 4th October, 1956 and 4th September, 2002 shall be verified to ascertain their genuineness and the persons possessing such land must prove

that such transfer was carried out legally to the sub-collectors concerned by04/09/2004. Those who don't provide such proof shall be treated as illegal encroachers and the land shall be restored to the original tribal owners.

- Persons in fraudulent possession of tribal land shall be liable of fine up to Rs. 5000/- and two years of rigorous imprisonment.

In non scheduled areas, the Orissa Land Reform Act, 1960 (Section 22 and 23), also forbids the transfer of *pattas* (Record of Rights (ROR), land by a Scheduled Tribe person to any person who is not a Scheduled Tribe, unless written permission is obtained from the competent authority. The OLR Act, 1960, also provides for penalty of Rs.200 per acre per year of land held illegally under this section. The dramatic protection provided in Scheduled areas under the amended OSATIP Regulation, 1956 as amended in 2002, has not been extended to the non-scheduled areas where protection to tribal land is provided by the Orissa Land reforms Act, 1960. Certain executive measures have also been made. The government has also issued notifications for the settlement and lease of waste and encroached lands in the state in which SC and ST has been given first and second priority. They are required to file applications before the local tahsildars for the allotment of such lands. Further, the Orissa Land Reforms Act, 1960, provided for permanent, heritable and alienable rights on land for the tiller. It started with a initial ceiling of 33 standard acres, then reduced it to 20 standard acres in 1965 and 10 standard acres in 1972. However this was met with resistance by big farmers who manipulated records to escape land ceiling provisions. Therefore, tenancy laws have been weak in Odisha. The tenants have found it very difficult to prove their possession of land as large landholders resort to rotating informal tenants among their holdings and periodically evicting them to escape the provisions of the law. The major effect of the tenancy laws has been to drive tenancy underground, making it more insecure and exploitative (Mearns and Sinha 1999).

Further, Odisha, has been witness to large scale displacement and land alienation of tribals in several projects like the Rourkela Steel Plant, NALCO at Damanjodi and Angul, NTPC at Kaniha; multi-purpose projects like Hirakud in Sambalpur, Machhkunda in Koraput and Salandi in Keonjhar districts (Majhi, 2009). For Rourkela Steel Plant, land acquired was much more than required, where the excess land was leased out to builders. More injustice as far as tribals are concerned is seen where compensation given to tribals is much less than what is given out to non-tribals. Best example can be cited from NALCO in Damonjodi, where displaced tribal people were given Rs. 2,700/- per acre while their non-tribal counterparts in Angul received Rs. 25,000/- per acre (Majhi, 2009).

As a result, today the tribals are disillusioned with the government and particularly with its neo-liberal strategies where tribal lands and forests are being forcibly grabbed by the state in the name of "development" for setting up industries, mines and Special Economic Zones (SEZ). This has not only threatened the livelihoods, religious and cultural rights of these groups but has driven them to utter poverty and misery. Therefore, present upcoming projects like Posco India Limited, Vedanta Aluminium Limited, L.N. Mittal Steel limited have faced stiff resistance from local and tribal communities[13]. In fact, Mittal has already withdrawn from Odisha, while recent reports say that Posco which has not become operational depite signing of memorandum with Government of Odisha in 2005, has decidedto withdraw from the State. Vedanta operation in Lanjigarh in Kalahandi district has halted by the unanimous decision of 12 gram panchayats in Rayagada and Kalahandi districts. This historic decision was possible because of the landmark Forest Rights Act, 2006.

As a result of these protests the Land Acquisition Act(1894) was amended in 2013 with an urgent need to check 'land grabs' to bring about inclusive growth in the country. Howerver, it still continues with the "public purpose clause" based on *'eminent domain'* , introduced by the British, later adopted by the post-colonial *'developmentalist state'* and today by a neo-liberal state. The doctrine of *eminent domain* refers to the power to take private property for public use by a state, municipality, or private person or corporation authorized to exercise functions of public character, following the payment of just compensation to the owner of that property. Forceful land acquisition in India can be traced to British colonialism. The British adopted an exploitative land and revenue policy and forcefully acquired land on a large scale particularly in tribal areas.

Land for generations has been regarded both as an economic and also a social commodity. As mentioned earlier land distribution in India is inequitable. Around 43 percent of rural households in the country are landless. Poverty in India, is linked to the absence of land rights to a vast majority of rural and tribal population. The Scheduled Caste (SC) and Scheduled tribes (ST) are however most disadvantaged as far as possession of land is concerned. This has resulted in high poverty levels among scheduled groups. This has made them more vulnerable to social injustice and exploitation. The state-corporate nexus today has further threatened them off their lands, homes and livelihoods in the name of 'development' where forceful land dispossession is for private corporation, real estate being described under the 'public cause' of LARR.

Many of the industrial projects have not been able to take off like Posco, and some have had to shut down operations like Vedanta. These cases, along with Kalinganagar have become symbols of resistance, where local communities have protested against their establishment and continuance. As a result, forceful land acquisition in Odisha for "development purpose" has acquired national as well as global attention. With its vast diversity of natural resources, like forest land, tribal land, mineral resources and long coastline, major contestation of interests over land have risen between the state and local communities.

NOTES

1. Earlier version appeared as "Land Acquisition and Tenancy Laws: A Study of Tribal Rights in Odisha" (2015) in *Tenancy Laws and Practices : Emerging Issues* (eds) Dr. A.A.A. Faizi, Dr. K. Gopal Iyer et al, Centre for Rural Studies, LBSNAA, Mussoorie) p. 323.
2. In early 20th century tribal movements were mostly agrarian in nature. Gradually they spread over the major tribal districts of Odisha, Bihar, Madhya Pradesh, West Bengal and revolved around the issues of land alienation and exploitation by non-tribals, egs, the Santhal Agitation (1937-40) in Purnea, Bihar; Munda Rising (1936-39) in Sundargarh, Odisha; Tanjore Revolt

in Tamil Nadu (1946-49); Tebhaga Movement (1946-47) in West Bengal.

3. Scheduled Areas are areas with majority tribal population, to which special provisions for protecting tribal identity, culture and interests are applicable under schedule V of the Indian Constitution.

4. Panchayati Raj Institutions (PRIs): The 73rd Constitutional Amendment of 1992 has been a landmark development as far as local self government in India is concerned. It has institutionalized three tiers of local government at district (usually called Zilla Parishad), block (various local names e.g. Taluk Panchayat, Panchayat Samiti, Mandal Praja Parishad), Panchayat Samiti (at Block or taluk level) and Gram Panchayat (at village levels) collectively called Panchayati Raj Institutions (PRIs) (Refer Mallik, 2011).

6. Schedule V areas are areas with with majority tribal population, to which special provisions for protecting tribal identity, culture and interestsare applicable under Schedule V of the Indian Constitution.

7. "Tribal" here refers to those communities notified as "Scheduled Tribes" by the President under Article 242 of the Constitution. There are more than 250 distinct tribal communities in India, amounting to about 8% of the total population.

8. Forest dwelling Scheduled tribes means the members or community of Scheduled Tribes who primarily reside in and who depend on the forests or forest lands for bona fide livelihood needs and includes the Scheduled Tribe pastoralist communities. Other "traditioanl forest dwellers" means any member or community who has for at least three generations prior to the 13th day of December, 2005 primarily resided and who depend on the forest or forest land for bona fide livelihood needs (FRA, 2006).

9. The name of the state was changed from Orissa to Odisha, and the name of its language from Oriya to Odia, in 2011, by the passage of the *Orissa (Alteration of Name) Bill, 2010* and the *Constitution (113th Amendment) Act, 2011* in the Parliament.

10. In exercise of the powers conferred by the sub-paragraph 6 of the Fifth Schedule to the Constitution of India, the revised Presidential Order titled "The Scheduled Areas (states of Bihar, Gujarat, Madhya Pradesh and Odisha) Order 1977'has declared the full districts of Mayurbanj, Sundargarh, Koraput (which now includes koraput, Malkangiri, Nabarangpur, Rayagada)

and six districts partly covered; Sambalpur, Keonjhar, Khondamal, Ganjam, Kalahandi and Balasore.

11. Under the Zamindari system, land was held as an independent property and revenue was assessed on the individual or community that owned the estate. The Zamindars (rich landlords) organised their own revenue collection agencies and often involved more levels of intermediaries. Under Ryotwari (peasant proprietary) the land belonged to the British Crown and was held in a right of occupancy, both heritable and transferable, by individuals. The revenue was assessed on individuals who were the actual occupants of smaller holdings and this was collected by the village headman whose office was hereditary.
12. One Standard acre is defined as in the Orissa Land Reforms Act, 1960, as unit of measurement of land equivalent to one acres of Class I land (irrigated land with two or more crops a year), one and a half acres of class II land (irrigated land with one crop a year), three acres of Class III land (unirrigated land used for single crop of paddy) and four and a half acres of class IV land (any other land).
13. Posco is a Korean iron and steel multinationl company with the highest foreign direct investment in the country. It signed a MoU with Government of Odisha in 2005. Vedanta is London-based multinational, a unit of NRI billionaire Anil Agarwal-led Sesa Sterlite.

4

Odisha: A "Poor Rich" State[1]

The present chapter analyses that despite being one of the most mineral rich states Odisha remains one of the poorest states of India. In the light of continuous farmers suicide cases in Odisha in recent years (2015-16), this paper argues that development strategies towards heavy industrialization by both national and international multi-national companies to exploit natural resources to overcome poverty has resulted in forceful land acquisition from already small, poor farmers mainly tribals, creating more poverty and greater social inequalities. This has led to an increase in state-society conflict and the stalling or closure of several mega-projects in the country. This argument is substantiated by case studies of Posco in Jagatsingpur district. Kalinganagar, Jajpur district and Vedanta in Kalahandi in the following chapter. The chapter argues that in an economy where agriculture continues to be the largest employer and the backbone of the country, damaging the backbone will weaken the State and lead to uneven development. Industrialization is needed to stimulate economic growth but growth needs to be balanced with human happiness and not at the cost of the poor.

4.1. ODISHA: A BACKGROUND

According to the Economic Survey Report of Odisha, 2014-15, Odisha constitutes about 4.9% of India's total area and 3.6% of total population as per 2001 Census – its density of population at 236 per square kilometre is lower than India's 324. In current prices, the per capita net state domestic product at Rs.22,630/- in 2007-08 is 68% of India's per capita net national product. Compared to all India average, the share of agriculture in gross state domestic product is relatively greater (25% to 19%, 2005-06), share of forest area to total area is greater (37% to 22%, 2002-03), net sown area to total reported area is lower (37% to 44%, 2002-03), net area irrigated to net sown area is lower (23% to 40%, 2002-03), fertilizer consumption is lower than half (2004-05) and yield of rice is less than three-fourths (2003-04) of the all India average (Government of Odisha (GoO), 2008). Workforce composition of 2001 suggests that 65% are dependent on agriculture (30% cultivators and 35% agricultural labourers) whereas it is 58% for all India.

Odisha has been among the poorest states in the country. It can be described as "the poor rich state". Poor because based on the NSS data and Tendulkar Committee Methodology, the poverty head ratio (i.e., percentage of people below poverty line) remains high for Odisha vis-à-vis India from 1973-74 to 2011-12 represented in Table 4.1.

Table 4.1

Poverty Head Count Ratio (Percent) for Odisha and India, 1973-74 to 2011-12

Year	*Odisha (%)*		*Total*	*India (%)*		*Total*
	Rural	*Urban*		*Rural*	*Urban*	
Expert Committee Methodology						
1973-74	67.28	55.62	66.18	56.44	49.01	54.88
1983	67.53	49.15	65.29	45.65	40.79	44.48
Tendulkar Committee Methodology						
1993-94	63.00	34.50	59.10	50.10	30.80	45.30
2004-05	60.80	37.60	57.20	41.80	25.70	37.20
2009-10	39.20	25.90	37.00	33.80	20.90	29.80
2011-12	35.69	17.29	32.59	25.70	13.70	21.92

Source : Economic Survey, Odisha, 2014-15, pp 7/2.

The high incidence of poor among scheduled tribes and scheduled castes and in southern and northern regions are matters of concern. Understandably, agricultural and other labourers in rural Odisha and casual labourers in urban Odisha have a greater incidence of poverty. What is worrying is incidence of 46% for poor among those self-employed in agriculture. Those self-employed in non-agriculture also have a greater incidence than the all India average and for urban Odisha the self-employed have a greater incidence than the state average.

However, agriculture remains a major employer with a majority of small and medium farmers. An examination of handholdings as seen from Fig 4.2 for the year 200-2001 is that large farmers comprise only 0.3 % operational holdings while marginal, small, semi-medium and medium constitute 56.4%, 27.4%., 12.3% and 3.6% respectively. This again reitetrates my argument that agriculture sector is very weak in the state. Incidence of poor by size-class of land indicates a greater burden among marginal and small farmers. This indicates that Odisha's rural households largely consist of marginal and small farmers (57%) and landless (36%) as shown in Table 4.2.

Table 4.2

Distribution of Operational Holdings in Odisha, 1990-91 to 2000-01

Size-class	*1990-91*		*2000-02*	
	Operational holdings (%)	*Area (%)*	*Operational holdings (%)*	*Area (%)*
Marginal	53.6	19.7	56.4	22.7
Small	26.2	26.9	27.4	30.4
Semi-medium	15.2	29.5	12.3	26.5
Medium	4.7	19.1	3.6	16.1
Large	0.4	4.8	0.3	4.3
Total	100.0	100.0	100.0	100.0
Total value*	39.48	52.96	40.67	50.81
Gini	0.4456		0.4318	

Source: GOO (2007) and www.indiastat.com

Thus, Odisha with a weak agricultural base, rich mineral resources, remains one of the poorest states of India Incidence of poverty, despite a decline remain much higher at 32.59 %, than the India average of 21.92% (Table 4.3). Although there is a decrease from 2009-10 of 37% to 32.59 for 2011-12, which is impressive but remains among the highest in the country at 32.59 % followed only by Bihar at 33.34 % as seen in Table 4.3 highlighting the incidence of poverty in Odisha vis-à-vis other states.

Table 4.3

Incidence of Poverty in Odisha vis-à-vis other States, 1973-74 to 2011-12

Sl No.	*States*	*1973-74*	*1993-94*	*2004-05*	*2009-10*	*2011-12*
1	Andhra Pradesh	48.86	22.19	29.90	21.10	9.20
2	Bihar	61.91	54.96	54.40	53.50	33.34
3	Gujarat	48.15	24.21	31.80	23	16.43
4	Haryana	35.36	25.05	24.10	20.10	11.16
5	Karnataka	54.47	33.16	33.40	23.60	20.91
6	Kerela	59.79	25.43	19.70	12.00	7.05
7	Madhya Pradesh	61.78	42.52	48.6	36.70	31.65
8	Maharashtra	53.24	36.86	38.10	24.50	17.35
9	Odisha	66.18	48.56	57.20	37	32.59
10	Punjab	28.15	11.77	20.9	15.9	32.59
11	Rajasthan	46.14	27.41	34.4	24.8	14.71
12	Tamil Nadu	54.94	35.03	28.9	17.1	11.28
13	UttarPradesh	57.07	40.85	40.9	37.7	11.26
14	West Bengal	63.43	35.66	34.3	26.7	19.98
	All India	**54.88**	**35.97**	**37.2**	**29.8**	**21.92**

Source: Odisha Economic Survey, 20014-15, pp7/5.

Further, a sectoral analysis of Odisha's economy shows according to Economic Survey, Odisha (2014-15), indicates a structural shift in the State economy, from agriculture towards industry and services sectors in the decade. As per 2014-15 (advance estimates), share of the Services sector (as per CSO classification) is expected to be about 51.2 percent of the Gross State Domestic Product (GSDP) followed by those of the Industry (33.4 percent) and the Agriculture (15.4 percent) in real terms at 2004-05 prices as shown in **Fig. 2.** The growth patterns also exhibit similar trend at All India level. The high growth rates recorded by the State in the 10th and 11th Five Year Plans were mainly due to high growth registered by the industry and services sectors. The performance of the agricultural sector continues to be highly volatile mainly due to adverse impact of natural shocks such as cyclones, droughts and floods.

Fig. 2. Sectoral Composition of Odisha's Economy 2014-15 at 2004-05 prices (in percent)

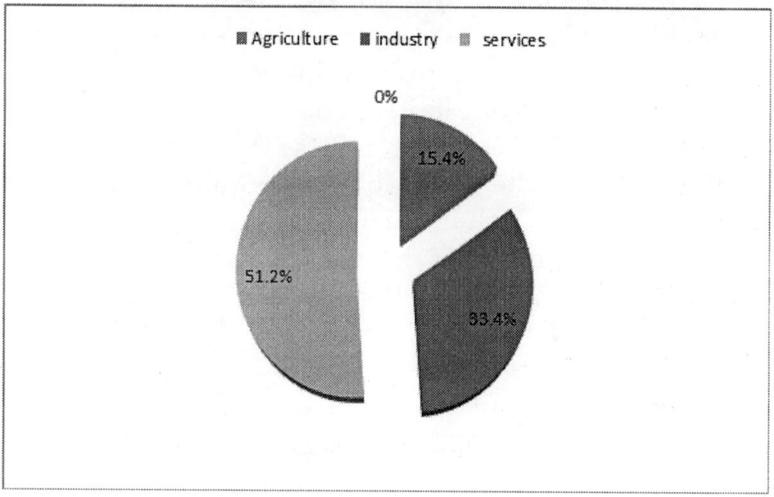

Source : Odisha Economic Survey (2014-15)

This sectoral shift has been in the context of the State following the New Economic policies enunciated at the Centre in 1991. The Government of Odisha adopted economic reforms, liberalizing the investment environment, adopting policies and regulations to remove institutional hurdles to unable private investors the right space for investments. This resulted in structural changes wherein there was a shift from an agrarian economy to an industrializing one. This led to a transformation in the economy from "agriculture based" to "industries and service sectors driven". As a consequence of these strategies the state government signed around several MoUs with mostly private companies to reap the rich mineral reserves of the state. Therefore, it is now important to examine the industry sector based on mineral resources of Odisha.

4.2 The Industry Sector

For the purpose of the survey, the industry sector consists of manufacturing, mining andquarrying, electricity-gas-water supply and construction sub-sectors. The sector contributedabout 33.45 percent share of Odisha's GSDP in real terms as per the estimates of 2014-15. In spite of global economic slowdown, disruption and other problems in the mining andquarrying sub-sector the advance estimate for the sub sector shows a growth rate of 2.30 percent in 2014-15. Most large-scale industries in Odisha are mineral-based. A look at the mineral wealth will justify my argument that Odisha is a poor rich state. The main minerals deposits in Odisha are represented below in Fig. 3. Coal reserves amount to 86%, Iron ore amounts to 7%, Bauxite and limestone 2%, while others constitute 3%.

It may be observed that about 59.67 percent of coal has been extracted in Anugul district and the rest from Jharsuguda, Sundargarh and Sambalpur districts. Iron ore extraction is mostly confined to Keonjhar district which accounts for 71.1 percent of total extraction, followed by Sundargarh (25.5 percent). Most of the bauxite mining takes place in Koraput district, followed by Rayagada (refer map of Odisha p. 62).

Fig.3 Minerals Reserve in Odisha, 2013-14

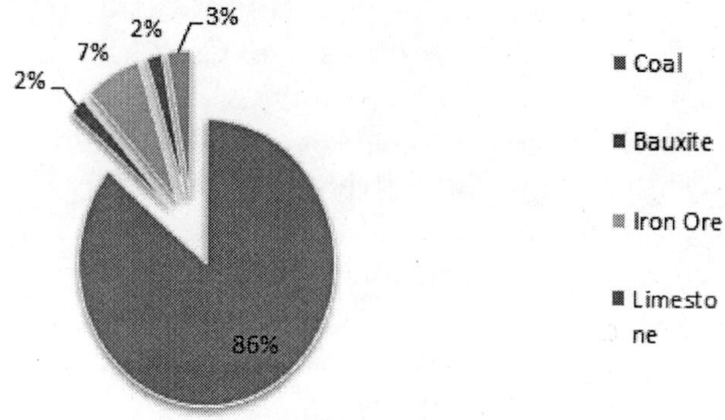

Source: Odisha Economic Survey, 20014-15

As regards a State-wise scenario during 2013-14, the value of mineral production (excluding atomic and minor minerals) from Off-Shore region was the highest at Rs. 54435 crore or 24.1% of the total value of mineral production followed in order of importance by Rajasthan Rs. 24714 crore or 11.0%, Odisha Rs. 22932 crore or 10.2%, Jharkhand Rs. 20645 crore or 9.1%, Chhattisgarh Rs.19566 crore or 8.7%, Gujarat Rs.12389 crore or 5.5%, Andhra Pradesh Rs. 11867 crore or 5.3%, West Bengal Rs. 11751 crore or 5.2%, Assam Rs. 11153 crore or 4.9%, Madhya Pradesh Rs. 11077 crore or 4.9%, Maharashtra Rs. 6899 crore or 3.1%, Tamil Nadu Rs. 6075 crore or 2.7%, Karnataka Rs. 5742 crore or 2.5% and Uttar Pradesh Rs. 3234 crore or 1.4 percent. Other States/Union Territories shared the remaining 3179 crore or about 1.4% of the total value of mineral production. Odisha stands second only to Rajasthan (11%) at 10.2 % in mineral production (*IBM, Govt of India*). The state has 25% of total iron ore reserves of the country and is also the largest almunium producer in India. Thus because of its rich mineral resources, Odisha has become the chosen destinations of both national and international multinational corporations (MNCs) like Posco, Vedanta, Tatas, Mitthal to name a few. A pro-industry approach welcomed these projects, believed to remove poverty and generate growth in Odisha. Thus heavy industrialization has been seen as the panacea to poverty eradication. The following Table 4.4 highlights the list of mega-projects signed in Odisha amounting to a whopping amount of Rs. 108,586 crores.

Table 4.4

List of Mega Steel Plant Project in Odisha as on November, 2005

Sl. No.	*Company*	*Location*	*District*	*Capacity million ton per annum*	*Investment Crores in Rs.*	*Year of MoU*
1	Tata Iron and Steel	Kalinga Nagar, Duburi, Jajpur	Jajpur	6.0	15,4000	2004
2	Sterlite Iron and Steel	Palasponga, Keonjhar	Keonjhar	5.1	12,502	2004
3	Hygrase Pellets	Paradeep, Jagatsingpur	Jagatsingpur	4.0	10,721	2005
4	Posco-India	Paradeep, Jagatsingpur	Jagatsingpur	12.0	51,000	2005
5	Jindal Steel and Power	Deojhar, Keonjhar, Angul	Keonjhar, Angul	6.0	13,135	2005
6	Bhusan Steel and Strips	Meramundali, Dhenkanal	Dhenkanal	3.0	5,828	2005
7	**Total**		**36.1**	**108,586**	**2005**	

Sources: *httl:/orissagov.nic.in*

However, despite rich source of minerals, and heavy

industrialization to overcome poverty, the State lags behind in Human Development Indicators (HDI), compared to other states of the country, which have low levels of heavy industrialization but are high up in Human development indicators, as seen in the following section.

4.5 HUMAN DEVELOPMENT INDEX IN ODISHA

Human development is a process of enlarging people's choices. But human development is also the objective, so it is both a process and an outcome. Human development implies that people must influence the processes that shape their lives. In all this, economic growth is an important means to human development, but not the end. Human development is the development of the people through building human capabilities, by the people through active participation in the processes that shape their lives and for the people by improving their lives (UNDP, 1990).

Pakistani economist Mahbub ul Haq created Human Development Index (HDI) in 1990 which was further used to measure the country's development by the United Nations Development Program (UNDP, 1990). The HDI is a summary measure of average achievement in key dimensions of human development: a long and healthy life, being knowledgeable and having a decent standard of living. The Human Development Index (HDI) is a composite statistic of life expectancy, education, and per capita income indicators, which are used to rank countries into four tiers of human development.[2]

The HDI is a measure for assessing progress in

three basic dimensions of human development: a long and healthy life, access to knowledge, and access to a decent standard of living. The HDI is the geometric mean of normalized indices for each of the three dimensions as shown below:

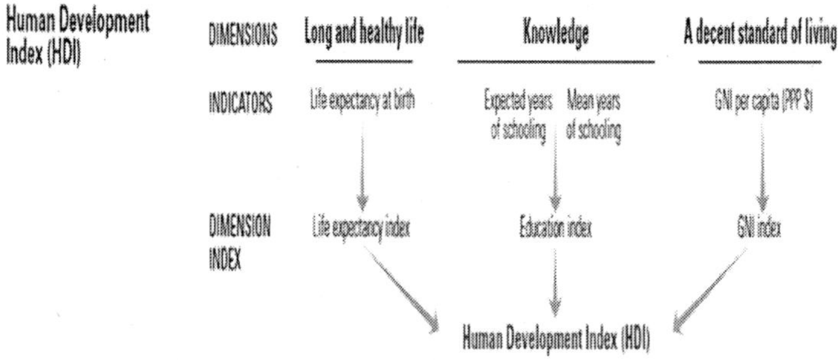

Source: UNDP, 2016.

Every year UNDP ranks countries based on the HDI report released in their annual report. HDI is one of the best tools to keep track of the level of development of a country, as it combines all major social and economic indicators that are responsible for economic development. India slipped down one place from 130 to 131 among the 188 countries ranked in terms of human development, says the 2016 Human Development Report (HDR) released by the United Nations Development Programme (UNDP, 2016).

India's human development index (HDI) value of 0.624 puts it in the "medium human development" category, alongside countries such as Congo, Namibia and Pakistan. It is ranked third among the SAARC countries, behind Sri Lanka (73) and the Maldives (105), both of which figure in the "high human development" category.

Since the 1990s a pro-industry approach, has not

been successful in removing inequalities in education, health, income distribution which have a crucial bearing on economic growth as well as on the final income distribution profile (HDR 2012-13). According to Human Development Index (HDI) and the Inequality-adjusted Human Development Index (IHDI) estimates of states in India, as shown in Table 4.5, the Human Development Index (HDI) is lowest for Odisha (0.444), followed by Bihar (0.447) and Madhya Pradesh(0.451). HDI is highest for Kerala (0.625), followed by Nagaland (0.609) and Mizoram(0.581) (HDR 2012-13, pp 239).

Table 4.5

Estimated HDI and IHDI across States

State	*HDI*	*IHDI*	*HDI Rank*
Andhra Pradesh	0.485	0.332	19
Arunachal Pradesh	0.527	0.356	13
Assam	0.474	0.341	20
Bihar	0.447	0.303	26
Chhattisgarh	0.458	0.297	24
Gujarat	0.514	0.368	15
Haryana	0.545	0.375	8
Himachal Pradesh	0.558	0.403	5
Jammu& Kashmir	0.525	0.371	14
Jharkhand	0.470	0.312	21
Karnataka	0.508	0.353	18
Kerala	0.625	0.520	1
Madhya Pradesh	0.451	0.290	25
Maharashtra	0.549	0.397	7
Manipur	0.556	0.400	6
Meghalaya	0.539	0.400	10

Mizoram	0.581	0.450	3
Nagaland	0.609	0.444	2
Odisha	0.442	0.296	27
Punjab	0.569	0.410	4
Rajasthan	0.468	0.308	23
Sikkim	0.5333	0.375	11
Tamil Nadu	0.544	0.396	9
Tripura	0.510	0.358	16
Uttar Pradesh	0.468	0.307	22
Uttarakhand	0.531	0.356	12
West Bengal	0.509	0.360	17
India	0.504 (world Average is 0.624)	0.343	Medium Human Development Countries

Source : India Development Report, 2012-13, pp 239

The relative ranking of all states highlights the following factors.

- Kerela is the only state in the country which remains in 'Very High HD' with respect to all dimensions, followed by Nagaland, Mizoram, and Punjab which fare well in most of the indicators.
- BIMAROU states (Bihar, Madhya Pradesh, Rajasthan, Odisha, Uttar Pradesh), and the states formed in 2000 (Jharkand, Chattisgarh, Uttarakhand) and Assam belong to 'Low HD' group, by almost all indicators.

An interesting observation that can be made from above statistics is that poverty is high in states with heavy industrialization projects, located in the mineral rich states as seen in Fig. 4.3. But these states comprise the BIMAROU states with low HDI. Therefore, it can be concluded that mineral extractive heavy industrialization is not the panacea to poverty in poor backward states like Odisha. Rather, there are alternative answers by which inclusive development can be worked out so that local communities become part and parcel of development policies and thereby do not resist the strategies that are being forced on the people. As seen from above data, Kerela, one of the smaller states of India is a shining example.

4.6. KERELA'S DEVELOPMENT EXPERIENCE

Kerela has received global attention from development economists on what has been now viewed as the "Kerela Model" or "Kerela's Development Experience" (Balakrishnan, 2015: 34). It has one of the lowest poverty levels and best social indicators in the country. The uniqueness of Kerela lies in the fact that, it has been able to combine a lowering of poverty with a wide spreading of social developments (ibid). Adopting from Balakrishnan's work, Kerala was one of the poorest states in the 1970s but it had attained the best social indicators in the country by then. This was popularized by Sen (Sen, 1999) wordwide and raised the question on "what is development?". Studies have shown that remarkable achievement comparable not only to China, but also to many advanced industrialized countries of the West (Sen, 1999: Dreze and Sen, 2002).

It is now well established that this success could be achieved by a focussed public policy which took the form of investments in health and education in the public sector. Added to this was another very significant development after the formation of the state in 1956. This was a programme of land reforms. This compared to other state in India, was more successful as it could significantly abolish tenancy and provided agricultural labourers title deeds to their land, up to a minimum of three cents on which their hutments stood. This, in one stroke, "abolished landlordism in its most gripping form" (ibid:32). This hardly left anyone in the countryside without land, if not for agricultural purpose but for the purpose of security. This marked a shift from feudalism to capitalism, thus creating a dynamic agricultural economy.

These reforms accompanied by investments in education and health by the state and directed towards women have been central to Kerela's achievements. Sen has describes this as 'building capabilities', which he describes as development itself (Sen, 1999).

Thus, the Kerala experience is an eye opener to mineral rich but most poor states that heavy resource extractive industrialization which threatens land and livelihoods of thepoor, will help to bring about growth and development in backward economies.

Ths study will now focus on the case studies of Posco in Jagatsinghpur district; Kalinganagar in Jajpur and Vedanta in Kalahandi district, in the subsequent chapter.

NOTES

1. Earlier versions of this chapter titled 'Industry and Rural Development with Reference to Odisha' was published in Productivity, National Productivity Council of India (NPC), Ministry of Commerce and Industry, Government of India (GOI), 2016, pp 149.

2. The Human Development Index (HDI) is a statistical tool used to measure a country's overall achievement in its social and economic dimensions. The social and economic dimensions of a country are based on the health of people, their level of education attainment and their standard of living. Pakistani economist Mahbub ul Haq created HDI in 1990 which was further used to measure the country's development by the United Nations Development Program (UNDP). Calculation of the index combines four major indicators: life expectancy for health, expected years of schooling, mean of years of schooling for education and Gross National Income per capita for standard of living. (*Economic Times)* The world's top three countries in HDI are Norway (0.949), Australia (0.939) and Switzerland (0.939).

5

State-Society Conflicts in Odisha

In order to tap the plentiful mineral resources in the State, the Government of Odisha promulgated the Industrial Policy Resolution in 2001 which helped in reducing the barrier for entry of national and international players into the sector. Posco, Vedanta and Kalinganagar have been the result of this policy. However, all three have become sites of state-society conflicts, where local populations whose existing livelihoods have been threatened, have resisted these development initiatives of the government. This chapter shall deal with these conflicts

CASE STUDY I : POSCO, PROJECT, JAGATSINGHPUR

(Profile of the Project, affected area and people)

5.1 JAGATSINGHPUR DISTRICT

Enriched with glorious cultural heritage, Jagatsinghapur district was formed on 01.04.1993 vide Govt. of Odisha notification No. 14218/R dated 27.03.1993 and EOG No. 459 dated 01.04.1993. Prior to this, it was a part of the erstwhile Cuttack district.

Jagatsinghapur district is surrounded by Bay of Bengal in the East, Cuttack district in the West, Kendrapara on the North and Puri district in the South (Refer Map).

Map of District

The district has an area of 1,759.00 Sq. Km with a population of 1,136,971. With a male population of 577,865 and a female population of 559,106, Jagatsinghpur has a sex ratio of of 967 female for every 1000 males, and a literacy rate of 87.13% (2011 Census). The Scheduled Caste population stands at 248,152 while the Scheduled Tribe population is 7,862.

Administrative Set up

Jagatsinghapur, a coastal district of Odisha, is situated

at a distance of 74 Kms from state headquarters Bhubaneswar and linked with both road and rail. The district is constituted of one Sub-Division with the same name. For the convenience of revenue administration, the district is divided into 8 tahasils namely Kujang, Tirtol, Balikuda, Jagatsinghapur, Ersama, Naugon, Raghunathpur, Biridi with one Tahasidar in charge of each tahasil. For development of rural areas consisting of 1294 villages in 194 Gram Panchayats, the district is divided into 8 Community Development Blocks with one Block Development Officer in charge of each Block.

Table 5.1

Block wise number of Panchayats and villages

Sl. No.	*Name of CD Blocks*	*No. of Gram Panchayats*	*No. of villages*
1.	Kujang	27	174
2.	Tirtol	27	249
3.	Balikuuda	30	237
4.	Jagatsinghapur	29	166
5.	Ersama	25	210
6.	Naugon 16 90	16	90
7.	Raghunathpur 19 87	19	87
8.	Biridi	21	81
	Total	194	1294

(Census of India, 2011)

According to 2011 Census, Jagatsingpur has a population of 1,136, 606. It has a population density of 681 inhabitants per square kilometer (1,760/sq m). Its population growth rate over the decade 2001-2011 was 7.47 %.

Socio-economic status of Jagatsingpur district

The economy of the Jagatsinghpur district is dependent on agriculture. Agriculture is the main occupation of bulk of the population. The key crops of the district are paddy, sugarcane, turmeric, cotton and jute. Processing, manufacturing, reparing and fisheries industries also contribute towards the economic development. Jagatsinghpur is a leading district of the state in terms of industrialization. Paradip, a modern deep water port, was built here in the 1960s and has now become a hot business destination due to the large foreign direct investment. The port town of the district has already emerged as the one of the country's major investment hot spot by attracting investment in excess of the tune of 3.5 lakh crores (US $68.84 billion) including the Rs 2, 74,134 crore Petroleum Chemicals and Petrochemical Investment Region (PCPIR) which has spread over 284 square kilometres (110 sq mi) in the area. IOC has already installed a 15 MMTPA refinery cum petrochemical complex at Paradip. Indian Railways has also taken up the Paradeep-Haridaspur 82 km broad gauge line to boost the infrastructure in the region. Up-gradation of NH-5(A) is also going on in a very fast rate. A new all green field road will also be built from Bhubaneswar to Paradip.

The following Large and Medium sector industries exist in the district. (GoO Portal, 2017)

- Paradeep Phosphates Limited, a fertilizer company
- Paradeep Plastic Park Limited
- IFFCO-Fertilizer Plant

- Essar Steel's Pellet plant
- Indian Oil marketing terminal
- Indian Oil Corporation Limited (IOCL) Refinery
- Bharat Petroleum Corp. Ltd. marketing terminal
- Hindustan Petroleum Corp. Ltd. marketing terminal
- Cargill's edible oil plant
- Skol Breweries Ltd. (Unit-East Coast Brewery)

5.2 POSCO–INDIA PROJECT AND ODISHA: A BACKGROUND

In addition to the above, another major entrant in 2005 was Posco, which met with stiff local resistance . This project was stalled and finally Posco has made its exit from the state in July 2017, marking a victory of the people' movement versus corporate greed. The study shall now turn to this state-society conflict.

Odisha had only two iron and steel plants until 1995. Growth in the iron and steel sector remained marginal from 1995-2000, but saw a rapid spurt in the post-2000 period. By November 2005, the BJD-led Government in Odisha had signed 40 MoU in the iron and steel sector as shown in Table 5.1. Of these six (including Posco-India) were mega steel project all above 3 MTPA (Million Tons Per Annum) capacity. The Odisha Government modified its own industrial policy in March 2007 in order to attract investigators. The policy created a framework of governance structure with the sole purpose of speedy and easy establishment of industrial projects (Ashar, 2009). The provisions of the MoU with Posco, included transfer of huge amount of land, raw materials, water and the right of establishing a new port at Paradeep. The MoU with Posco was signed without considering the impact on the lives and livlihoods of the local population of this region. It therefore, turned into a nightmare for 22,000 people from the affected panchayats of Dhinkia, Gadakujang and Nuagaon (Padhi & Patana, 2017).

On 22 June 2005, the Biju Janata Dal (BJD) Government in Odisha signed a Memorandum of Understanding (MoU) with the South Korean multinational corporation and the World's fourth largest steel producer, Pohang Steel Company (Posco), to construct a $12 million tonne per annum (mtpa) steel plant integrated steel plant in the in the Erasama block of Jagatsingpur (MoU, 2005). This was at an estimated cost of Rs. 52,000 crore, hailed as the largest foreign direct investment in the country. Along with the steel plant, the company was to source iron-ore from the Kandahar mountains spanning across the neighbouring districts of Sundargarh and Keonjhar. and a captive port at the mouth of the Jatadhari river. The area of operation of the proposed plant would span over three panchayats namely Nuagaon, Dhinkia, and Gadkujang with a land requirement of a massive 4004 acres of which 3000 acres were marked as forest land. The project was a matter of pride to the government of Odisha which declared that the project would "bring prosperity and well-being to its people and generate about 8.7 lakh jobs for 30 years".

The steel plant was one of many coming up in Odisha, which has adopted a policy of rapid industrialization through a "steel revolution", to overcome poverty and backwardness. This was based on one of the key developments in mineral sector under the economic reforms in India, the Mines and Mineral (Development and regulation Act), 2015 and National Mineral Policy of 1993. This brought amendments to the Mines and Minerals Act 1957and set deregulation of the mining sector by allowing 50 % investment of the foreign companies in mining and opening all non-atomic minerals to private investment.

National Mineral Policy of 1993 evolved as a result of the economic reforms introduced by the government in 1991. This was a major step in encouraging private sector and foreign direct investments in the mineraral and mines sector. This opened the doors for thirteen minerals namely iron, sulphur, gold, manganese, diamond, cupper, chrome, nickle, tingsten and platinum reserved for the public sector to the private sector and foreign investors. It was only in 2006 that the goverment, based on the recommendation of the Anwarlal Hoda Committee, opened the mining sector fully to foreign investments, thus paving the way for the entry of multinational corporations (Planning Commission Report, 2012)

In 2015, the MMDR 1957 Act was amended (Mines and Minerals Development and Regulation Act), which had introduced a provision for reconnaissance permits, providing the states the right to grant leases for exploiting the minerals and raised the cap on foreign direct investment to 100%. Given the rising metal prices, mineral rich states like Odisha started aggressively attracting both domestic and foreign investment into this crucial sector.

5.2.1 PROVISIONS OF MoU

According to the MoU, Posco would invest Rs 52,813 crore to build a 12-MTPA (Million Tons Per Annum) capacity steel works and develop mines and linked infrastructure over three phases from 2007 to 2016. Posco would set up an integrated steel plant at Paradeep in Jagatsinghpur district with an annual production capacity of 12 million tonnes of steel. It would also establish an Indian Company through its relevant subsidiaries or third parties (to be nominated by Posco) to invest in the state of Odisha in: (a) steel manufacturing, (b) infrastructure necessary for the integrated steel plant and related projects and (c) related mining of iron and other related ores in Odisha. The MoU involves supply of non-renewable mineral and fuel resources, water, and land to Posco, the facility of construction of a new port at Paradeep if necessary and various other incentives and concessions including recommendation of "Special Economic Zone (SEZ)" status to Posco as a "SEZ Unit". Further, Posco would also get chrome and manganese ores from Orissa Mining Company (OMC) and the quantity of these ores to be given to Posco, was not mentioned in the MoU. It would also get limestone and dolomite at concessional rate. Coal is another important raw material for steel production, which Posco would be provided by Odisha Government. The Odisha Government also agreed to supply water to Posco plant at Paradeep from Jobra barrage of river Mahanadi. One important aspect of this MoU also to provide facility if needed to Posco for construction of a new port at Paradeep. Posco will also be provided with 6025 acres of land, out of which 4000 acres will be for construction of steel and related plants, 20-25 acres for its office and 2000 acres for establishing a big township. In order to make this MoU more meaningful the Odisha Government agreed to construct railways and roadways for providing transport and communication facilities to Posco. Another provision of the MoU is to recommend to the Government of India to declare the plant and other related project areas as a "Special Economic Zone (SEZ)" to strengthen functioning of the company. Thus in essence as a result of this MoU, Posco would be the owner of iron ore, coal mines, steel plant and related projects with freedom to export 100 per cent of 12 million tonnes of steel produced per year, port and dock facilities and the status of "SEZ" (*Memorandum of Understanding between the Government of Odisha and M/S Posco for establishment of An Integrated Steel plant at Paradeep at http://www.orissa.gov.in/posco/Posco-MoU.htm*)

The land area details of Posco are given below in Table 5.2.

Table 5.2

Land Area Sought to be Acquired by Posco

Purpose	*Location*	*Extent/Scope*
Steel Plant: 12 Million Tonnes Per Annum (mtpa)"green field"	Erasama Block, Kujang Tehsil, 10 kilometers from Paradeepport, 7 revenue villages, 2 hamlets, 3 Gram Panchayats (Nuagaon, Dhinkia and GadaKujang)	4004 acres of which 3000 areclassified as "***forest land***"

Mines: 600 million tonnesreserved over 30 years (20million tonnes per year)	Khandadhar Hills (Keonjhar and Sundergarh districts)	Prospecting Lease (3applications), Mining Lease (2applications) submitted byPosco; 2500 hectares Khandadhar hills; no clear territorial demarcation– only textual claims in government recommendation
Township	At steel plant and at mines 2000 acres (1500 at steel plant, 500 at mines)	2000 acres (1500 and steel plant)
Water	Jobra Barrage of the Mahanadi River	3.50 cubic meters per second(cumecs)

Sources: *Posco office*, July 2014.

The proposed plant area was located about 15 kms from Paradeep port. The district administration has identified 1877 villages growing betel vines on 309 acres of government land to be removed and compensated. Thereafter,the government started a forcible land acquisition. However, this was being done without environmental clearance from the Ministry of Environment and Forests (MoEF).

Based on the recommendations of the Saxena Committee which reported that the State government had violated the Forests Rights Act, 2006 (FRA, 2006), the assistant inspector general of forests, MoEF, called for a stoppage of all land acquisition in a letter to the state government on August 5th, 2010. The state government opposed this and Chief Minister Naveen Pattanaik called for the intervention of then Prime Minister, Manmohan Singh. The Centre appointed another Committee under former Environment

Secretary, the Meena Gupta Committee, to probe FRA violations by the state government. Despite differences between the committee members, there was broad agreement in the Committee that the procedure to recognise forest rights should be re-done in the project villages

As far as resettlement and rehabilitation is concerned, the committee felt ththat though nothing can compensate for the trauma of displacement, the R and R package is a good one, better than the norms laid down in the Odisha Government's Resettlement and Rehabilitation Policy. However, landless labourers received very limited benefits even though their livelihoods were affected. Further, it needs to be ascertained whether fishermen, have fishing rights along the coast and in the area of the Posco project, and if not, they need to be compensated. The Committee members felt that higher compensation should be paid for the paan plots, but basically they felt that the forest land should not be diverted at all. (Meena Gupta Report, 2010).

However, three distinguished members of the committee, tribal affairs expert Urmila Pingle, former director general of forests, Devendra Pandey and Madras High Court advocate V. Suresh – have pointed out that Ms. Gupta's recommendations "are not only untenable but legally impermissible". They wanted to scrap all environment and forest clearances for the South Korean giant. They prepared another dissenting report (*The Hindu,* 2010). According to this, the three members questioned Ms. Gupta's argument –that the Posco case must be treated differently from Vedanta because it did not involve tribal communities. They both "Posco and Vedanta are alike in the sense that in both instances there is gross violations of law with impunity," they said, terming the argument discriminatory and diversionary. "It is indeed strange to say that the rule of law should be followed only for tribals and if the project is already underway, but the same can be overlooked and condoned if the project affected are the Scheduled Castes (SCs) and fishing community who according to us are also equally vulnerable and exploited sections of society.... It is most unfortunate that the interests of the two most vulnerable sections of our society - SCs and STs - are being pitted against each other in order to favour corporate interests." However, after dithering for almost four weeks after discussing the Posco proposal the Forest Advisory Committee (FAC) finally made up its mind to reject the clearance due to violations of the Forest Rights Act (FRA).

Thus, Posco remained a stalled project and was finally withdrawn from Odisha in 2017. A few families who had taken compensation and moved to rehabilitation centre have returned back to their villages; others whose betel vines were demolished have started rebuilding their vines and livelihoods. Therfore, an understanding of the MoU will throw light on the Posco resistance.

5.3 STUDY AREA

The present study was conducted in Nuagaon, Dhinkia, Govindpur and Gadkujang village under Ersama block. Dhinkia, Govindpur come under Dhinkia panchayat, Nuagaon and Gadkujang come under Nuagaon and Gadakujang panchayats respectively.

Fig 4

Maps of Proposed POSCO Project in Odisha

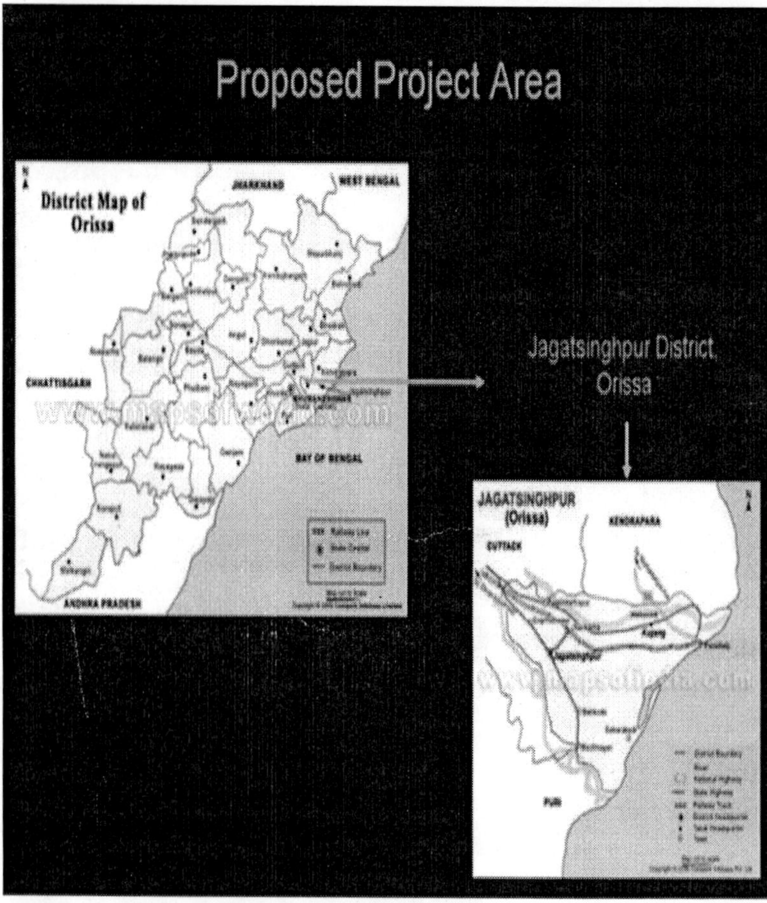

Source: *www.jagatsingpurdistrictmap.nic.in*

Nuagaon and Gadkujang village is at a distance of around 41 km from Cuttack district head quarter and 20 km away from Jagatsingpur district head quarter. This district is subdivided into 8 tehsils, they are Jagatsingpur, Kujang, Tirtol, Balikuda, Biridi, Nuagaon, Erasama and Raghunathpur.

The study interviewed residents from the above villagers namely, Nuagaon, Gadkujang, Govnidpur and Dhinkia, seven revenue villages comprising 11 hamlets in three gram panchayats (Nuagoan, Gadkujang and Dhinkia). In all, 571 households (HHs) were interviewed, from the four mainly affected villages and hamlets like Nuliasahi and Bhuiyapal and Polang. Focus group discussions were held with the hamlet populations which have regular meetings in the panchayat office. Data was collected from the following villages:

1. Gadkujang village (Gadakujang Panchayat): - 62 HHs (Nuliasahi 135 HH and Bhuiyapal-12HH, Polang -62) -209 HHs
2. Dhinkia village (Dhinkia Panchayat: - 162 HHs
3. Gobindapur village (Dhinkia Panchayat)- 90 HHs
4. Nuagaon village (Nuagaon Panchayat) - 110 HHs

The land acquisition for Posco is from these panchayats as mentioned above namely: Nuagaon, Gadkujang, Govindpur and Dhinkia. In Nuagaon 32.99 % comprise private land while 67.08% is government land. Similarly, in Gadakujang it is 14.92% private land while 85.08 government land; in Dhinkia it is 33.16% private while 65.83% government; and in Govindpur it is 26.26% private and 72.54% government land.

The four main affected panchayats have a total population of 14,427 and total HHs are 2626. A break–up of occupation of these HHs shows agriculture is 9.56 %, betel vine cultivation 28.23 %, fishing 3.12 %, landless labourers 58.73%. The area consists of mainly small and marginal farmers with an average landholding size of 1.00 to 2.5 acres. However landless labourers belonging to mainly SCs comprise around 63 % of the population. They are engaged as labourers in paddy cultivation of landowners or in the betel vines. Very few have their own betel vines comprising of only 2%. An additional estimated 20,000 to 25,000 people from 30 neighboring gram panchayats would suffer loss of their livelihood as fishermen and betel vine farmer because of the proposed Posco port (field study, 2015).

Although in case of Posco there is less land acquired from farmers, it poses a very difficult situation. This is because the site lies very close to the sea, and remains prone to cyclones and flood. Further, every year sea water runs into the fields damaging paddy. Therefor, in the absence of alternative security, farmers have started cultivating betel vines, as it is suited to the soil and climate type of this area. Further, betel is grown of raised land as fresh sand is put every year before cultivation, thereby raising the land. This prevents the salt water from damaging the crop, thus making betel vines the main source of livelihood of the people of this area.

5.4 LAND ACQUISITION BY POSCO

Local leaders of the anti-Posco movement say the entire population will be affected by the project. It is interesting to note that the protest principally seems to be centred around the acquisition of private agricultural or other land by the government and also on the diversion of forest land. This is because many of the villagers cultivate *paan* or betel vine on the forest land, and earn a good income from it. The *paan* grown is reportedly of the expensive variety.

The land classified as forest is consists mainly of casuarinas, planted after a major cyclone in 1971. There are also some cashew and other trees and shrubs. The vegetation, other than the casuarinas plantations can, at best, is described as scrub forest. However it is very good land for cultivating *paan*. The people in the villages falling in the project area besides cultivating paan on the forest land, also collect cashew and some other forest produce and fuel wood from this area. There is a difference of opinion on how long the paan cultivation on the forest land has been going on. Some of the villagers claim that it has been going on from the time of their forefathers, from the days when the land was part of the Bardhaman Estate, others claim that the cultivation started about 20 to 30 years ago. The villagers, are now considered as encroachers by the Government as their rights on this land have not been recognized so far or settled. According to MoU, land to be given to Posco from the villages of the above panchayats is shown in Table 5.3.

Table – 5.3

Land availability of Posco affected village

	Panchayats	*Number of households*	*Land in acres*		*Total land in acres*
			Govt land including forest land	*Private land*	
1	Nuagoan	726	928.68	480.01	1408.69
2	Gadkujang	647	907.63	864.56	1772.19

3	Dhinkia	703	1338.56	284.97	1623.53
4	Govindpur	550	910.21	344.52	1254.74
Total		**2626**	**4085.08**	**1974.06**	**6059.15**

Sources: primary data

The above Table 5.2 shows the details of the land required from the four panchayats. There are 2626 households, 4085.08 acres of government land including forest land and 1974.06 acres of private land. Of these 928.68 acres of forest land and 480.01 acres of private land belongs Nuagaon panchayat. Gadkujang pachayat consists of 647 households having total 1772.19 acres of land in which 907.63 acres of lands are forest land the rest 864.56 acres of land is private land. In these two panchayats betel vine cultivation is carried out on Government land. Dhinkia panchayat consists of 703 households, 1338.56 acres of forest and 284.24 acres of private land. This panchayat has the highest amount of forest land as compared to others three panchayats. Govindpur panchayat consists of 1254.74 acres of land in which 910.21 acres of land belongs to the government land and rest 344.52 acres of land belongs to private land.

The compensation package by Posco was a payment of Rs. 17 lakh per acre of agricultural land while the price of area under beetel cultivation was fixed at 11.5 lakhs (TOI, 8th July, 2010). The company also agreed to pay Rs 2,250 per month to people cultivating beetel vine on government lands. It also agreed to provide a job to one member of every displaced family according to their education and qualification. The company also announced Rs. 2 lakh per acre used as fish ponds according to the new rehabilitation package announced at the Rehabilitation and Peripheral Development Agency Committee (RPDAC). Also it would built a three room pucca house built on 10 decimal land with a cowshed for each displaced family.

The State government was much elated with this deal and the project. The National Council of Applied Economic Research (NCAFR) conjured up an estimated "8.7 lakh jobs for 30 years" as employment that the project would generate.

However, this package though accepted by a some, was rejected by majority who did not wish to part from their land and livelihoods in return for some monetary benefits. Thus this project was resisted by the local communities. This turned into a nightmare for the local communities when the state administration with the help of the police force forcibly occupied land damaging beetel vines, the main livelihood of the people.

5.4 THE RESISTANCE MOVEMENT

Betel vine cultivation is the major source of livelihood for the people in these panchatyats giving them a good income. It is more lucrative than paddy cultivation. This is because this area is regularly affected by cyclones and sea water floods the fields. However, as betel is cultivated on raised grounds and are well sheltered from strong winds, it has become a main source of livelihood in this area. Hence the resistance to land acquisition by Posco as the compensation will not sustain them forever and also if they are displaced they will not get such type of land for the betel vine cultivation. Hence, they are totally opposed to the Posco project in this area. The government conducted a palli sabha to take a majority opinion of the villagers on the Posco project on 21st February 2011, where they unanimously opposed land acquisition for Posco. Some protestors said, they do not want Posco to come up in our fertile land which is gives them *'dhana'* (paddy), *'panna'* (betel) and *'mino'* (fish). Another villager Jiban Behera told, "we have taken a vow to fight against the project till our last breath. If the Government uses force on innocent people, bloodshed would take place".

A total of 1119 betel vines spread across, have been demolished from the three pa namely Nuagon, Kadakujanj and Govindpur. No vines have been demolished from Dhinkia which has become the core of the resistance movement, as the entire village is involved in its cultivation. Table 5.4 shows the total number of betel vine on government land in acres demolished for the Posco plant. This completely devastated the economy of these areas affecting the livelihood of the communities. There was a decline of household incomes.

Table – 5.4

Total number of betel vine demolished for the Posco plant (Only Govt. land)

Name of the Panchayat	*Total number of betel vine Destroyed*	*Percentage*
Nuagaon	486	100
Gadkujang	165	100
Dhinkia	00	00
Govindpur	468	100
Total	**1119**	

Sources: R.I. Nuagaon circle on 19/08/2015

There was a decline of household incomes.Table 5.5 shows an average monthly household income before land was acquired by Posco was Rs.5,000 to 7,000, from betel vine cultivation. All the families member are engaged in betel vine farming. The women also made an income through plucking of betel leaves. After government acquired land for Posco, their households monthly has dropped down to Rs.1, 000 to 2,000 and presesntly they are facing a lot of hardships to survive. With the betel vines destroyed, and land taken over by the state and handed to Posco, the promised job in the plant nowhere in sight, these local communities are therefore resisting the setting up of Posco. Most of the affected people are working as a daily wage labourer in and outside the village. But work is also not available daily which has led to severe hardships to survive.

Table – 5.5

Average households annual income from betel vine

Sl. No.	*Village name*	*Betel vine cultivation In acres*	
		Before acquired land in Rs.	*After acquired land in Rs.*
1	Nuagaon	5,000-7,000	1,000-2,000
2	Gadkujang	5,000-7,000	1,000-2,000
3	Govindpur	5,000-7,000	1,000-2,000
3	Dhinkia	8000-10,000	Not taken land

Sources: primary data.

5.5 AN ANALYSIS OF POSCO CONFLICT

As seen from the survey, the affected villages namely Nuagon, Kadakujanj and Govindpur and Dhinkia under the three panchyats of Nuagon, Gadakujanj and Dhinkia, are located in Jagatsingpur district in Ersama block, at a distance of 15kms away from Paradeep Port. As mentioned earlier this district and this block were the worst hit when the super cyclone hit Paradeep port in 1999.

These villages have a population of around 55% Scheduled castes who are mostly agricultural labourers, followed by other backward castes (12%) and general caste (33%). This area does not have a Scheduled tribe population. The literacy level amoung SCs and OBCs is low around 27 %. The average land holding is from 1.5 to 2.0 acres, which is mostly possessed by the general category. This area being close to the sea is affected by cyclonic low pressures in the sea every year. Paddy cultivation is also affected by saline water flooding of the fields. Thus paddy cultivation which is done in winters is not sufficient to sustain the villagers. Therefore they have taken up betel cultivation. Betel leaf is popularly known as *paan,* is an integral part of Indian society. It is grown in the tropics and sub-tropics for its evergreen leaves that are used in religious functions and also as a chewing stimulant across the country.

The climatic conditions and soil in this area is very suitable for betel cultivation. Betel is grown in well drained soil, raised higher than the adjacent areas, in closed cultivating systems, covered by straw and coconut leaves, which provide good shade as seen in the picture below:

Betel cultivation in closed cultivating systems, Dhinkia village, 2016

Paan cultivation is extremely lucrative and as seen in the field survey, provides an average monthly income of around Rs. 7000-8000. It also gives the villagers the freedom to lead their lives amidst nature on their own terms and not be an employee of a company. This was highlighted by the villagers in their discussions with the researchers. Even women are engaged and are involved in plucking of leaves. Thus, betel or *paan* cultivation is the lifeline and the most profitable means of livelihood in an otherwise low paddy production and a cyclone –prone area. Besides their economic potential the betel vines groves are revered as temples. The social cultural fabric of the villagers revolves around the betel groves or *paan bareja*.

Therefore although land acquisition of private land by Posco is small compared to government land, the resistance to Posco is because of the damage to betel vines, on which the local communities thrive and meet their livelihood needs. According to.Jeebanlal Behera, a villager, farmers are cultivating betel vine as primary crop, throughout the year. According to one estimate there are 5,000 betel vineyards grown in the area's three Gram Panchayats, which are tended by 10,000 cultivators. A single betel leaf sells for 1.0 rupees, and farmers often enjoy strong profits from cultivating betel vine gardens. For example, a garden of 100-150 vines in Jagatsinghpur district produced an annual profit of about Rs. 2,00,000 in 2010. Thus a majority of small farmers and also the landless started betel cultivation and have been doing so for generations on government land.

Posco Office, Burnt by the affected villagers of Nuagaon, ON 15/03/2015, source: Field work, 02-04-2015

CASE STUDY-II

TATA STEEL PROJECT

(Profile of the Project, affected area and people)

The Kalinga Nagar Industrial complex is another attempt made by the Government to expand the industrial base of the state and to utilize the untapped mineral resources in Jajpur district of Odisha. Jajpur district comprises of 6 Tehsil namely, Binjharpur, Darpani, Dharmasala, Jajpur, Sukinda and Bari. Out of the six tehsil, Sukinda is located in relatively hilly and undulating terrain and is famous for huge deposits of chromite ores within its boundary. Lot of mining and industrial activity is taking place in most parts of the area under this tehsil.

5.7 INDUSTRIAL COMPLEX AT KALINGANAGAR

Kalinganagar is a geographical unit consisting of a compact landmass of Danagadi and Sukinda Blocks. The plant is the largest amoungst a list of plants alloted in the Kalinganagar complex by IDCO. Table 5.6 shows the list of plants in Kalinganagar.

Table 5.6

List of plants and land allotted in Kalinga Nagar

Sl No.	*Name of the Plants*	*Land allotted (in acres)*
1	MESCO	530
2	Orion	150
3	Maithan Ispat	100
4	Uttam Gala	370
5	NINL	2500
6	Maharastra Seamless	500
7	TSL	2400
8	Rohit Ferrontech	50
9	JSL	678
10	Visa Industries	390
11	Dinabandhu	100
12	K.J. Ispat	50

Source: *ADM office Kalinga Nagar..* (Mesco-Mideast Integrated Steel Limited; NINL- Neelachal Ispat Nigam Limited; JSL-Jhindal Steel Limited; TSL- Tata Steel Limited).

This geographical area is being developed by Odisha Industrial Infrastructure Development Corporation (IDCO) where the Government of Odisha aims at developing a steel-producers-hub. IDCO has acquired the land from public, has developed infrastructure and has given it to various industries for setting up steel plants. The process has started since the early 1990s and the former chief minister, late Biju Patanaik, took the lead role in promoting the steel-hub. Later, the industrial activity grew when Naveen Patnaik became the chief minister of Odisha. Now there are around 15 steel plants which includes public sector plant like NINL, private sector plant like JSL, Mesco etc. Tata Steel has set up its steel plant here.

The Tata Steel at Kalinga Nagar is one of the five mega steel, plants that are to be set up in the State. The area falls within Danagadi and Sukinda block of Jajpur district. (www.jajpurdistrict.nic.in) as seen in map below.

Fig 5

Map of Jajpur district

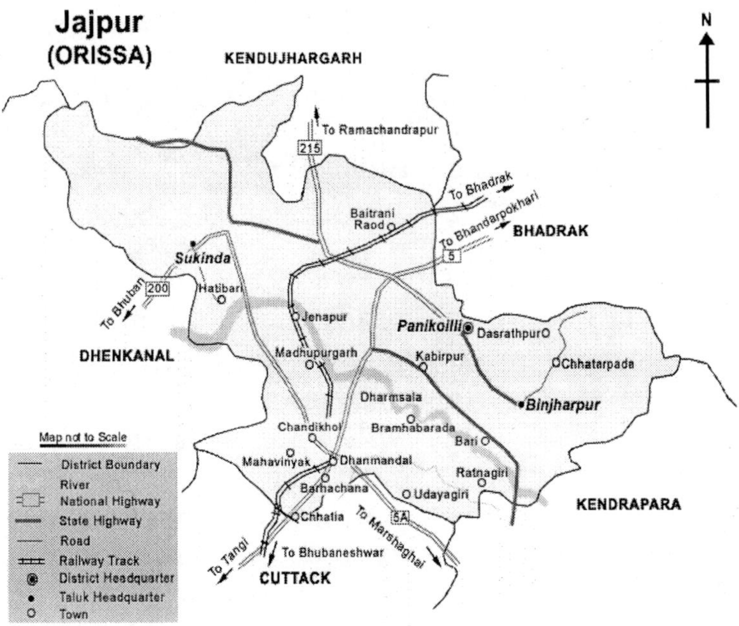

Sources: *www.jajpurdistrcitmaps.nic.in (Fig -5)*

The acquisition of land by IDCO for Kalinganagar Industrial Complex began in early 90s in different phases with the advent of liberalization and economic reforms initiated in the country. IDCO was entrusted by the government to develop infrastructure facilities to create an industrial hub to attract private investors. The Odisha government has signed several MoUs with several industrial houses. Tatas have been one of the main investors who have signed a MoU in 2004 to set up a 6MMTPA steel plant in two phases, with an annual investment of Rs. 154000/- million (MoU, 2004).

5.8 LAND ACQUISITION AND AFFECTED COMMUNITIES

The land acquisition which was started by IDCO in the1990s acquired about about 13,000 acres by 1st of January 2006. Of these, 6900 acres were private land and the rest was said to be 'government land'. However in reality people were cultivating most of these 'government land' for generations for which they had no record of rights (ROR) or *pattas*. The land survey and settlement in the area was not done since 1928. The Tata Steel plant's construction work is going on over a massive area of 2400 acres of land, and and has started operation since November 2015. All villagers are being displaced from their homestead land.

There are six villages which are being affected by the Tata Steel plant. These villages are Chandia, Gabraghaty, Gadapur, Baragadia, Khurunti and Nuagaon (Table 5.7). Out of six affected villages, Chandia comes under Danagadi block and rest five villages under Sukinda block. However, all the six villages are under the control of Kalinganagar police station located at Duburi town. Gobaraghaty, Chandia and Baragodia come under same Gram Panchayats. Gadapur and Khurunti come under Sarang Gram Panchayat and Nuagaon under Baragodia Panchayat.

Table-5.7

Administrative set up in the project area of Tata Steel Limited

Sl. No.	*Affected villages*	*Hamlets*	*GP*	*Police Station*	*Block*
1	Chandia	Chandia, San Chandia, Baidubari, Kalamatia, and Baligotha	Chandia	Kalinganagar (Duburi)	Danagadi
2	Gobaraghaty	Gabaraghaty, Sasagothasahi, Ambagodia, Bamiagotha and Champakolia	Gobara-ghaty	Kalinganagar (Duburi)	Sukinda
3	Gadapur	Bandargodia, Gadapur	Sarangpur	Kalinganagar (Duburi)	Sukinda
4	Baragadia	Harijonsahi, Toposahi, Damasahi, Baragodia	Baragodia	Kalinganagar (Duburi)	Sukinda
5	Khurunti	Siaria, Manpur, Khurunti	Sarangpur	Kalinganagar (Duburi)	Sukinda
6	Nuagaon	Nuagaon	Baragodia	Kalinganagar (Duburi)	Sukinda

Sources: Primary data.

During the early stage of TSL plant erection, there was public resistance to setting up of plant which led to police firing on 2 January 2006, killing 14 people and one policeman. Thereafter, the government brought policy changes and Company offered better Compensation and R&R package and propagated inclusive-growth model what they called as "TATA-Paribar-Scheme" for the affected people.

5.8.1 Displacement and Compensation

The majority population of the affected villages are tribals and small farmers mainly belonging to scheduled caste. Most of these communities have been cultivating the land for generations, but have no legal rights or are in possession of pattas. Here lies the bone of contention between these communities and the government, as the later only recognizes and compensates those possessing proper land titles. As per the information from various field visits to the area, initially the local population were not against industrialization. Rather, they supported the process as they were made to believe of a golden future. The protests started when they demanded compensation in the form of 'land for land', as monetary compensation does not give the same quality of life as before loosing their lands. Further, as the landless people were denied compensation, the Kalingnagar protests grew demanding compensationstion for them.

There are 1954 households of the six villages having population of 10,004. There are 311 households of Chandia with population of 1621, there are 558 from Gaabaraghaty having population of 3220. This is the largest village. There are 140 households of Gadapur, with a population of 852. There are 502 households in Baragadia, with a total population of 2416, there are 341 households of Khurunti, with a population of 1606 and only 82 households of Nuagaon village having population of 329 (Table 5.8). The population of all villages consists of 98% tribal population.

Table 5.8

Demographic Profile of the Village of the study area

Sl. No	*Village*	*No. of households*	*Population*			*Sex Ratio*
			Male	*Female*	*Total*	
1	Chandia	331	811	810	1621	999
2	Gabaraghaty	558	1750	1470	3220	840
3	Gadapur	140	421	431	852	1024
4	Baragadia	502	1252	1164	2416	930
5	Khurunti	341	849	757	1606	892
6	Nuagaon	82	166	163	329	982
	Total	**1954**	**5249**	**4795**	**10044**	

Sources: **Census of India, 2001.**

These six villages have already been displaced and resettled in four resettlement colonies, namely Gabaraghaty Birsa-Munda rehabilitation colony (ST people), Sansailo rehabilitation colony (mostly OBC people), B.R. Ambedkar Trijanga rehabilitation colony (mostly SC people) and New Champakoila rehabilitation colony (both SC and ST people). The field study was conducted on these affected families in the rehabilitation colony.

5.9 TATA STEEL AND AFFECTED POPULATION

As mentioned earlier, it has started its production from Kalinganagar Plant. Local displaced people (DPs), Project Affected People (PAP), periphery people are getting contract work and getting employment. In partnership with the Government of Odisha, Tata Steel is committed to set up a 6 million-tonne per annum integrated steel plant at Kalinganagar Industrial Complex at Duburi, in the Jajpur district. The steel works will be established in two modules of 3 million tonnes of steel each and when completed, will have a capacity of 6 million tonnes per annum (MoU). Special attention has been given to all the requirements of the families in rehabilitation colonies and resettlement camps that are fully equipped with all amenities. With Kalinganagar emerging as the steel hub of Odisha, Tata Steel will help boost the pace of industrialization and socio-economic development, not only in the State but in the country as well.

In 2012, Maniapatala village was added where 39 families are to be displaced, taking the total number of families to be displaced to 1234. As of December 15, 2012, 993 families (out of 1234 families) have relocated voluntarily in support of the project. Data was collected from 553 households.

Kalinga Nagar has a dominant tribal population along with dalit population. In the two blocks of Sukinda and Danagadi, 36.06 percent and 28.19 percent are scheduled tribes and 11.89 percent and 22.31 percent

are scheduled castes respectively. Of the tribes, *Ho* community constitutes nearly 80 percent of the population, and the rest of them belong to *Munda* and *Santal* community. These tribes are indigenous populations who have been residing in the acquired villages since two to three generations. Majority of *Mundas* are living in the study area. In fact contact and discussion with the aged persons of the community revealed that they had migrated from Keonjhar, Sundergarh districts to this place during first half of last century to earn their livelihood from mining activities in Sukinda area. Gradually they moved to periphery areas of Sukinda and settled here. Being landlessness, they were allotted land by kings of princely states or by the Government decades back (Ota, 2010). However, they possess no land records.

5.9.1 Socio-Economic Profile

An occupational breakup of the affected population shows that 8.82 percent of people depend on cultivation or agricultural activities. It is very less in number because only Sansailo and New Champakoila colonies have agricultural land. They purchased land by themselves. A majority of 28.08% are daily wage labourers, while 10.63 % are in the services of Tata steel. Women comprise 14.92 percent of the population and are engaged in the selling country liquor *(handia)* and liquor *(Mahua)* to add the the family income.

(Source: field study, 23-5-2015). The literacy level is also much lower for the STs compared to the SCs. The villages also have a high percentage of agricultural labour, around 37% compared to farners with land (8.82%).

Thus, a dominant tribal population ,comprising a majority of small marginal farmers and agricultural labour, with low literacy levels, were the worse hit by the Tata steel Plant.

5.10 PROVISIONS OF MoU

Memorandum of Understanding was made on 17th November, 2004 between Government of Odisha of the one part and The Tata Iron and Steel Company Limited of the other part.

(A) Land:

i. Tata steel will require approximately 2400 acres of land at Kalinga Nagar Industrial Complex, in the district of Jajpur, Odisha.

ii. The Government of Orissa agrees to hand over 2000 acres of land at Kalinga Nagar industrial Complex, immediately and remaining 400 acre subsequently free from all encumbrances to Tata Steel through Orissa Industrial Infrastructure Development Corporation (IDCO) for constriction of the plant and allied facilities.

iii. Further, the Government of Orissa/IDCO agrees to acquire and provide land to Tata Steel for development of Civil Township and infrastructure like road, rail link etc.

iv. For rehabilitation of displaced families, if any, Rehabilitation and Resettlement Package would

be implemented as per prevailing guidelines and practices of Government of Odisha.

v. Tata Steel agrees to pay IDCO the cost of land, contribution for development of common infrastructure, annual ground rent and cess as applicable.

(B) Raw Materials:

Coal- in case Tata Steel requires coal for the captive power plant as well as for the production process, State Government agrees to recommend to the Government of India for allotment of suitable coal block for captive coal mining for the project.

Iron Ore and Other Minerals:

Tata Steel has indicated that an integrated steel plant of the size of six million tonnes of steel per annum can be established only with the assured source of captive iron ore mines containing at least 250 million tonnes of reserves of iron ore. Tata Steel will construct township in the mining areas for its workforce for which land will be made available to Tata Steel by the Government of Odisha, as per rules.

(C) Water

i) The Government of Odisha will permit drawl of water from the Kharsuan river upstream of Jakoria barrage/ a suitable source of water for construction and operation of the aforesaid project and housing colony, as per the prevailing rates under appropriate terms and approval of the Water Allocation Committee.

ii) The Government of Odisha agrees that Tata

Steel may built necessary infrastructure including creation of water bodies, laying of pipelines etc. to pump required amount of water for the operation of the Steel Plant and township.

(D) Power

The Government of Odisha agrees to arrange for supply of power to the steel plant through GRIDCO/ Distribution licenses. The requirement for the steel plant of total capacity of 6 million tonnes will be about 322 MVA (289 MW) from the grid. The details of the year-wise build up of power requirement will be worked out by Tata Steel and Indicted to the Government of Odisha and GRIDCO/distribution licensee.

(E) Environment

The Government of Odisha agrees to assist Tata Steel in obtaining no objection certificate (NOC) through the State Pollution Control Board for the construction of the plant, the housing colonies, mines, water supply infrastructure; power projects etc. the Government of Odisha agrees to assist Tata Steel in obtaining all clearance from the Central Government.

(F) Incentives and Concessions

Tata Steel understands that the State Government would grant such incentives and concession as are provided in the relevant Industrial Policy Resolution (IPR) of the State Government.

(G) Railways, Roadways and Port

i) The Government of Odisha will assist in making

available necessary land for railway link from nearest railhead to the mines and steel plant for transportation of raw materials and finished goods. Tat Steel will pay for the cost of such land as per rules.

ii) The Government of Odisha will facilitate Tata Steel in Constriction of approach roads to the steel plant as well as connecting service roads to the iron ore and coal mines.

iii) In order to ensure that adequate port facilities are available within a reasonable distance from the steel plant, Tata Steel, in Joint Venture with Larsen and Toubro will build a deep water, all weather port at Dhamra capable of handling cape-size vessels. Towards this, Tata steel has signed on 29th October 2004, definitive Joint Venture Agreements viz. Share Subscription Agreement and share holder's Agreement with Larsen and Tubro to hold 50 percent equity in Dhamra Port Company Ltd (DPCL), which will build and operate the port at Dhamra.

(H) General Clauses:

i) The Government of Odisha appreciates that Tata Steel is a responsible corporate house with a high involvement in employees' welfare and social development. The Government of Odisha, therefore, anticipates that Tata Steel will bring this philosophy to the steel plant project being set up in the district of Jajpur to ensure the well being of this district in particular and the people of Odisha in general. In terms of employment, preference will be given to the persons of Odisha subject to need and their possessing the necessary qualifications. Tata Steel will make every effort to improve their skill levels, if necessary, through specialized training.

ii) Tata Steel agrees to affect sale of all its products of the Kalinga Nagar plant (including inter-state sales) in the State of Odisha. These stipulations are not, however, applicable to export of finished products outside the country. (MoU, 2004).

The present study has been carried out in the four rehabilitation colonies which are located at East, West, North and South direction of Duburi town. The study interviewed 200 households from the four rehabilitation colonies of Tata Steel namely, Gabaraghati Birsa-Munda rehabilitation colony, Trijanga rehabilitation colony, Sansailo rehabilitation colony and New Champakoila rehabilitation colony. The data was collected from the displaced people now residing in these colonies and the ADM office of Jajpur district. Mangal Singh Jamuda and Purna Chandra Soy, two activists, were also interviewed.

The affected villages have been rehabilitated in four rehabilitation colonies namely, Gabaraghaty Birsa-Munda rehabilitation Colony, Sansailo Rehabilitation colony, Trijanga B.R. Ambedkar rehabilitation colony, New Champakoila Rehabilitation Colony. (see pictures at the end of chapter).

5.11 KALINGANAGAR AND LAND ACQUISITION

As per the MoU signed between Govt of Odisha and Tata, 2400 acres of land at Kalinga Nagar Industrial Complex would be provided by The Government of

Odisha to Tata Steel through Odisha Industrial Infrastructure Development Corporation (IDCO) for constriction of the plant and allied facilities like for development of Civil Township and infrastructure like road, rail link etc. Further, the Government of Odisha/ IDCO agrees to acquire and provide land to Tata Steel For rehabilitation of displaced families, if any, Rehabilitation and resettlement Package would be implemented as per prevailing guidelines and practices of Government of Odisha.Tata Steel agrees to pay IDCO the cost of land, contribution for development of common infrastructure, annual ground rent and cess as applicable.

However, the crisis started in the 1990s. Keeping, in line with its industrial liberalizing policies, the state government, started acquiring land for the huge Kalinganagar Industrial Complex under the archaic Land Acquisition Act, 1894 The State government however used the "public cause" clause to acquire land from mainly tribals without any land records with a paltry compensation. This Act allows displacement for undefined public purpose, without the consent of the people affected and Odisha is still following this act. The acquisition of land, by IDCO for Kalinga Nagar Industrial complex, was mainly diverted to Tata Kalinganagar Steel Plant. About 13,000 acres of land has been acquired by the IDCO. Of this 6,900 acres are private lands, while the remaining 6100acres said to be 'Government' land which the tribals were cultivating for which they do not have any written evidences *(patta)*. The land survey and settlement in the area have not been done here since 1928. This acquisition was resisted by the Visthapan Virodhi Jan Morcha (VVJM), an protest organization

established in 2004. The climax of this movement reached on 2nd January, 2006 when the Tatas performed the bhumi puja to start construction of its plant, which was opposed by the local tribals. The police resorted to firing killing 13 tribals, which shook the nation.. and raised the 'development for whom debate'. The opposition was strengthened and continued till 2013 when Tatas got possession of the land and started construction of its plant. after a comprehensive compensation packet and the displaced people were 'rehabilitated and adequately compensated by the Tatas as given in Table 5.9.

COMPENSATION DETAILS

Table-5.9

Displaced family and the Rehabilitation Assistance is given below

Sl.No.	*Compensation of different things*	*In Rs.*
1	Land compensation	1,00,000 in acres
2	House building Assistance	1,50,000
3	Temporary Accommodation Assistance	10,000
4	Transportation Allowance	2,000
5	Cash –in-Lieu of job	2,00,000
6	Maintenance Allowance	2,300
7	Training and employment	Training and employment to nominated person

Source: *ADM office Kalinga Nagar, 22-12-2014.*

Tata Steel gave compensation to: households losing more than two-thirds of their agricultural land and entire land and entire homestead land shall receive Rs. 2 lakhs per family as compensation; families losing more than one-thirds, but less than two-thirds of their agricultural land and entire homestead land shall receive Rs. 1 lakh per family, while all other displaced families will get cash assistance of Rs. 50,000 per family. An assistance of Rs.10, 000 only shall be provided for each displaced families for the temporary accommodation assistance. In order to ensure timely evaluation, an allowance or Rs. 2,000 per month per displaced family shall be provided on vacation of land/house for a period one year and training and employment to nominated person.

Table- 5.10

Monthly income before and after displacement

Households monthly Income	*Before displacement Average monthly income In Rs.*	*After displacement Average monthly income In Rs.*
	2500-4000	8,000-10,000

Source: *Primary Data, 12-04-2015.*

Agriculture was the primary source of income for the majority of the people the area. People are primarily agriculturalists and some of them earn their livelihood as daily wage laborer. They collect forest products, like cooking wood, wood for the house making, leaf for the leaf plate. This is their subsidiary occupations.

as forest were very near to their home. Their average monthly income was Rs. 2500-4000 which they were getting from the agricultural land. After the displacement by the Tata Steel their households' average monthly income is increased that is Rs.8, 000-10,000. The villagers in the rehabilitation colonies are receiving health facilities from Tata Health Centre in Trijanga rehabilitation colony. However, they informed that the facilities were limited to first-aid only. Emergency cases were referred to Sum and Hitech Hospitals in Bhubaneswar around 120 kms away. The villagers also reported that two delivery cases lost their lives in this transit.

Health Centre in Trijanga Rehabilitation Colony

The health centre in Trijanga colony has two pharmacists, six community health providers and six Para medical staff. Apart from them, there are two doctors from Jajpur who visits the colony every Wednesday. An Ambulance is available 24 hours to serve emergency patients. Furthermore, the basic immunization facilities and immediate medical attention to the residents is provided at the health centre. In case of severe cases, they are referred to High Tech Medical College, Bhubaneswar.

Tata Steel Gobarghati hospital

The hospital in Gobarghati Rehabilitation Colony is set up on an area of four acres of land. The setting up of this hospital is primarily dedicated to those families that were affected in Tata Steel's Greenfield project at Kalinganagar, and also for the people in periphery villages. It is a 200-bed hospital and would cater to around 10000 people from the neighbouring villages apart from Tata Steel Parivar members.

However for the serious patient they are referring to Bhubaneswar, the costs of which are borne by Tata Steel.

5.12 ANALYSIS

However, despite Tatas rehabilitation and resettlement policies and the facilities provided the protest continues. The tribals who lost land received compensation and the associated facilities of rehabilitation. However, the rehabilitation of landless labourers has not been adequate. The rehabilitation colonies have been provided with a school, health facility and drinking water. Also as mentioned by the Research & Rehabilitation Head, they are getting 50 kg of rice, 5 kg of dal, kerosene and mustard oil etc. every month. The locals say the food, kerosene has stopped and the survival compensation that they were receiving have also ended. Very few have got employment in the industry

This highlights that the tribals and other local communities who were self-reliant have lost their livlihoods and now wait for food and basic requirements from the company or the government.

The sad part is that these people who were self-reliant, working in their own fields, deriving their livelihoods from land and forests are today beggars in their own land. They have no land(very few have acquired land elsewhere), and forest land has been diverted. They were promised training and jobs, but only few, particularly those with political clout or showing favour to the company have been rewarded. Majority are jobless. The majority (86%) said they have lost their agricultural land which was their *"Bhato handi"* (rice bowl). They were getting fire wood from the forest, leaf for the leaf plate, from the forests. The tribal women who are very significant part of the tribal economy are left without any source of livelihoods. Besides working on their own fields or on the fields of other, collecting kendu leves and forest products from the forests and selling them, the women are a significant part of tribal economy. Today they are lleft with no additional alternatives to add to the family income. and keep their own hearths burning. Thus it is seen that a further dependency of the local communities has been created instead of making them strong and self-reliant The dust from the steel plant has also damaged the small fields that some villagers still possess at a distance.

The Tata–Kalinganagar case has again highlighted that livelihoods of the tribals, poor farmers, agricultural labourers, have been threatened and they have to wait for support from the government or the Rehabilitation and Resettlement scheme of the company. Instead of mainstreaming the poor and the marginalized, the industrial project like other industrial projects in the country are creating centres of exploitation and further marginalization of the vulnerable. Their poverty is increasing where a new elite is created who is reaping the benefits of this process while vulnerable communities have to now wait for company dole outs,

Tata Steel plant (Source: Field work, 22-12-2014)

thus increasing their poverty and dependency. Thus as claimed by the government that the mega industries would generate employment opportunities and remove inequality stands challenged.

Project Fellow at the time of data collection

Gabaraghaty Birsa-Munda Rehabilitation colony, Source: Field work, 23-12-2014

Trijanga B.R.Ambedkar rehabilitation colony, Source: Field work, 23-12-2014

Sansailo Rehabilitation colony, Source: Field work, 23-12-2014

New Champakoila Rehabilitation Colony, Source: Field work, 23-12-2014

Worship place Jaher than of The Tribals of Gabaraghaty Birsa-Munda Rehabilitation Colony, Source: Field work, 17-07-2015

Kalinga Nagar Saheed Sthambha, Source: Field work, 17-07-2015

CASE STUDY- III

VEDANTA PROJECT, LANJIGARH AND DONGORIA KONDHAS

This study will now focus in Section I, Vedanta refinery set up at the foot hills of Niyamgiriri hills displacing mainly *Kutia Khondas*. Section II shall discuss the the Vedanta and the *Dongaria Kondhas* who resisted bauxite mining by Vedanta from the Niyamgiri hills, their sacred home. This was upheld by the Supreme Court of India, which in its ruling has stopped all mining rights of Vedanta from the hills.

5.13 KALAHANDI DISTRICT

Kalahandi is one of the thirty districts of the Odisha. Since 2nd October, 1992, the former Kalahandi has been re-organized into two districts viz., Kalahandi and Nawapara. As per the District Statistical data the landmass of Kalahandi district is 7,920 Sq. km representing 4.68 percent of the area of the State. It comprises 3.64 percent total population of the state. The literacy rate in the district is 62.45 percent as per 2001 Census. Scheduled Tribes constitutes 28.84 percent while Scheduled Caste constitutes 17.67 percent of total population of Odisha. It is one of the poorest districts in the country, well known for its droughts and famine.

Bamandeb dongar (1033 m) and Niyamgiri hill (1306 m) are the major elevated land features in the area. The valleys are mostly narrow and well dissected.

5.14 ADMINISTRATIVE SETUP

There are two-subdivisions namely Bhawanipatna and Dharamgarh and 13 blocks, 12 police stations. There is 273 Gram Panchayats which 2236 villages in the district. Blocks under Bhawanipatna sub-divisions are, Bhawanipatna, Kesinga, Lanjigarh, Narla, Karlamunda, blocks under Dharamagarh, sub-divisoin is Dharamgarh, Junagarh, Koksara, Jaipatna, Kalapur and Galamunda. The distrcict head quarter is Bhawanipatna. There are 13 Community Developmenty blocks comprising 273 Gram Panchayats and 2099 inhabited villages. (*District Statistical Handbook, 2011*)

5.15 INDUSTRIALIZATION IN KALAHANDI

Kalahandi happens to be a bowl of rich resources with regard to agriculture, mineral and minor forest produce. Kalahandi despite rich mineral resources and forest resources, continues to reel under poverty. Therefore the state government has launched as in other parts of Odisha, heavy industrialization to remove poverty .However, like the other projects as discussed above, there is a strong resistance by local communities, and in Kalahandi, the protest have been led by a particularly vulnerable tribal group (PVTG).

5.16 PHYSIOGRAPHY

The district can be divided into two district physiographic region: (i) the hill tracts and (ii) the plains. The hill belongs to the main line of the Eatern ghats and contains extensive platue of about 4,000 feet in elevation with long tropical grass grown over them. The hill-sides rising up precipitously from the plain is covered with sal forests. The valley areas between the hills tracts (locally called, Dongar or Dongorola) are fertile and cultivated in some portion with the help of perennial streams. (*District Census Hand Book, Kalahandi, Census of India, 2011.*)

Fig 6

Source: www.kalahandidistrictmaps.nic.in

Niyamgiri is a hill range, about 250 sq. km. in area (Daspatnaik, 1984) lying between 19.33 degree North longitude and 83. 25 degree East longitude (Patnaik, and Daspatnaik, 1982). It forms the northern most hills in the massive cluster of hills called the Niyamgiris or the *Dongaria Kondha* country. Also known as the Niyam Dongar, it runs in a southwest alignment with a maximum elevation of 1306 meters.

Niyamgiri Hills are better known as the country of 'Dongria Kondhs'. Dongaria Kondha is one of the Primitive and Particularly Vulnerable Tribal Groups of the State and enjoys a critical and symbiotic relation with the Niyamgiri forests. The Dongarias believe that the hill country belongs to Niyam Raja Penu, a male deity, who is worshipped during Dussera and *Jura parab* (festival of the *dongorias*). They claim themselves to be descendants of the Niyam Raja. The *Dongrias* have derived their name from *'dongar'* meaning agricultural land on hill slopes. If one claims to be a *Dongaria Kondha,* he must reside in the Niyamgiri hills and possess land of his own, and pass on to his posterity. The Dongrias have a distinguished heritage, because of their dress style, mode of living, indigenous skills, cultural pattern and social system interlinked with nature and forests. Both culturally and ecologically, the Niyamgiri hills are extremely rich and significant.

Most importantly Niyamgiri hills are the source of Vansadhara river as well as a major tributary of Nagavali river. It forms a distinct photo geographical zone because of its height and its highly precipitous topography. It also has some of the most pristine forests in Odisha, and is home to a number of vulnerable wildlife species including tiger, leopards, sloth bear, pangolin, palm civet, giant squirrel, mouse deer, langur and sambhar, etc. It is also on the path of migration corridor of elephants, and comes within the territory of Royal Bengal Tiger.

Source: Primary Vedanta Aluminium Plant, Lanjigarh, 15-03-2015

5.17 VEDANTA AND LANJIGARH

In 2003, Vedanta Resources signed a Memorandum of Understanding with the State Government of Odisha for construction of a refinery for aluminium production, a power plant and related mining development at Lanjigarh in Kalahandi district, Odisha. M/s Sterlite Industries (India) Limited (SIIL), fully owned and controlled by Vedanta Resources, proposed to set up a refinery with a capacity of 1.0 million Tonnes Per Annum (TPA) for processing Aluminium for export. It also proposed to extract bauxite from the area adjoining the refinery, which is estimated to have approximately 73 million tonnes of mineable ore.

Location

The plant site is about 3.7 KM from Lanjigarh. The plant is located on the road connecting state highway NH-6 (Bhawanipatna - Rayagada) to Lanjigarh. Small villages, agricultural lands and grazing lands, surround the site. Niyamdangar forms a topographical high land in the area with an elevation of 1300 m above MSL. Niyamgiri plateau (1210 m),

The current study has chosen six villages in Lanjigarh, among which four have been displaced and two others are going to be displaced by Vedanta Alumina Limited (VAL). The name of the displaced villages is Kinari, Borbhotta, Kothdwara and Chhatrapur. The whole village of Kinari has been displaced and being settled in the Rehabilitation Colony on the hill slope which as Dongar. The other three are partially displaced. Some of them have lost their agricultural land and house. The field survey has revealed that all the above four villages have lost their agricultural land. There were 826.56 acres of agricultural land taken from the four villages by VAL.

Field data also indicated that the two other villages mnamely Renopalli and Basantapada are going to be displaced.

The study interviewd 200 villagers from the different villagers namely, Kinari, Borbhotta, Kothdwara and Chhatrapur, Kothadwar, Bundel, Sindhbahal. Two Vedanta officials, two Sarpanch, two R.I. (Revenue Inspector) of Rayagada and Kalahandi, some villagers of Vedanta rehabilitation colony were also interviewed. The official statements or interviews of the former land acquisition officers have also been used as primary source of data collection.

5.17.1 Features of Vedanta Aluminum Limited (VAL)

The total distance from mine top to alumina plant is approximately 18 km. to construct access roads. To create the overburden dumping area and other infrastructure facility on the hill top, there is a proposal to remove trees on 30 hectares of forest land. The site inspection report of the Deputy Conservations Forests (Central) indicated that the total number of trees to be felled are about 21,337 from two forest dimension that is Kalahandi (41,296 trees) and Rayagada (80,041 trees). In mining lease area approximately 40 percent enumerated trees are situated which balance 60 percent are on access and other planted facilities.

The refinery required total 2007.72 hectares of land for the proposed expansion including the existing plant as before in 2007 (see Table 5.11).

Table-5.11

Land requirement and Expansion

Existing Land (1.0 MMTPA)

Purpose	*Acres*	*Ha*
Main palant	691.58	279.87
Red mud	452.06	182.94
Ash mud	235.79	95.42
Township	129.61	52.45
Railway	132.96	53.81
Total	1642	6664.49

Source: Report of Environmental impact Assessment (REIA) report, 2007

In 2007 it again required additional land to be acquired (about 1343 Ha) for accommodating the additional facilities of the plant, red mud pond, township and railway corridor. The land under acquisition was mostly barren land and un-irrigated. Care was taken not to acquire irrigated land. There is no homestead on this land. The additional land for the proposed expansion for an additional 6MMTPA production is in the eastern side of the refinery.

Land under reference covers a part of Lanjigarh village, under Lanjigarh police station limits of Kalahandi district, Odisha.

The study area covers an area of 227.02 sq km (22702.73 ha) within the circle by 10 km radius around the proposed plant site. In comparison with the satellite data, the wasteland and marginal areas of non-cultivable land are been utilized by the existing refinery and further the non-cultivable land were utilized for the expansion refinery, it has taken the forest land of 3172.95 hector which is 14 percent.

Table 5.12

The details of irrigated land, un-irrigated land use patterns

Sl.No.	*Particulars*	*Study Area (ha)*	*percentage*
1	Forest land	3172.95	14.
2	Land under cultivation	00	00
3	Irrigated land	427.08	1.9
4	Unirrigated land	9524.13	42
5	Cultivable waste land	3042.28	13.4

6	Area not available for cultivation	6536.29	28.8
	Total area	22702.73	100.0

Source: Report of Environmental impact Assessment (REIA) report, 2007

The Table 5.12 shows that the land structure of the studied area is having 3172 acres forest land, in the forest land most of the *Kutia Kondh* people are staying in the lower parts of the Mountain and in the upper parts *Dongoria Khond* is staying. Only 42708 acres of land are irrigated land and 9524.13 acres of un irrigated landfind in the study area that is consists of 42 percent of the total area. There are 3042.28 acres of lands are consists of wasteage land that is 8.8 percent of the brack up land area.

5.17.2 Socio-Economic Status of the Study Area

The socio-economic condition of the tribals in Lanjigarh is a matter of grave area of concern. They wage a continuous struggle for their daily survival and livelihood. Not withstanding their toil and hardship for subsistence, they live in abject poverty.

The study area covers Bandhuguda, Borbhatta, Kothdwara, Regopali, Jagannathpur, Balabhadrapur, Chhatrapur, Kinari, villages where mainly the scheduled tribe such as, Majhi, Kandha, Bonda etc. people are living. Some of these villages such as Chhatrapur, Balabhadrapur are at a stone's throw from the refinery and Vedanta Township. The socio-economic conditions of the tribal were mainly confined with the forest products as most of the areas were under the forest coverage and the Niyamgiri hill with deep forest. Next to their forest they were depending on agriculture and natural vegetation. They were having the fertile land and adequate production was there. When interview the villagers about the agricultural condition they strongly said that they had a good agricultural production before the Vedanta alumina limited.

The field study started in Vedanta Nagari located at near Vedanta Alumina Company plant where total 165 families were residing. There are total 249 people among which 119 are males and 130 are females as per the 2011 census data. In the village population of children with age 0-1 is 51 which make up 20.48 percent of the total population of the village. Average sex ratio of the village is 1092 which is higher than Odisha state average of 979. Child sew Ratio for the village as per census is 1318, higher than Odisha average of 941. The villages have a lower literacy rate compared to Odisha. In 2011, literacy rate of the village was 45.45 percent where male levels literacy stands at 68.04 percent while female literacy rate at 23.76 percent. (Table 5.13)

The displaced villages

The details of the villages which are displaced by the VAL are given below. The following Table 5.15 shows the villages displaced with their people and lands.

After that for the expansion of the refinery the VAL has applied for the environmental clearance assignment to the Odisha government. After its approval it is going to take more two villages which are given below in the following (Table 5.14).

Table 5.13

Socio-Economic Status of the Study Area

Sl. No.	*Name of the village*	*Area of the village (in ha.)*	*No. of H.H.*	*Total popu-lation*	*SC*	*ST*	*Sex Ratio male and Female As per 1000*	*Worker*			*Main Worker*	*Marginal worker*	*Literacy rate percentage*
								Total	*Male*	*Female*			
1	Balabhadra pur	94.70	156	618	101	136	1032	274	168	106	114	160	34.5
2	Bandhguda	38.45	65	249	123	99	915	100	50	50	60	40	45.45
3	Basantapada	41.28	170	735	16	317	1058	228	136	92	5	223	41.68
4	Chhatrapur	134.36	284	1013	504	65	963	473	275	198	330	134	62.99
5	Jagannathpur	400.64	730	2018	558	611	1172	1036	725	311	734	302	64.84
6	Rengopali	165.11	79	249	48	195	976	168	78	90	62	106	35.90

Source: Census Report 2011.

Table 5.14

Displaced Villages

Sl No.	*Name of the villages*	*Total population*	*Population displaced*	*Area of land taken by VAL (in ha.)*	*SC Individual*	*ST Individual*	*No. of Households*	*No. of houses displaced*
1	Kinari	72	72	35.25	9	24	32	32
2	Kothadwatr	114	114	65.36	92	17	28	28
3	Sindhbahal	218	122	69.61	79	139	50	41
4	Borbhatta	132	52	59.23	29	96	55	34
5	Bandhuguda	249	0	28.45	123	99	65	0
6	Bundel	144	0	35.39	6	150	39	0
	Total			293.29				123

Source: Census Report 2011

Table 5.15 The villages to be displaced

Sl. no	*Name of the villages to be displaced*	*Population*	*Land area household*	*Households*	*SC*	*ST*
1	Rengopalli	210	165.11	53	11.8%	88.2%
2	Bandhuguda	249	28..45	65	10%	90%

In the above two villages, mainly the *Kutia Kondh* are residing, whose lands will be acquired by the Vedanta Aluminum Refinery. In villages, *Kutia Kondh* and *dalit* households have sold their agricultural lands to the company and are left only with their homestead land. Officially, they are classified as Project affected Persons (PAPs) who have lost their agricultural land but not their homes.

According to the field data 121 families are resettled in the NVN colony. They were compensated at levels above the minimum required stipulation mandated by pertinent laws. Seventy six people have been employed and are on the company pay role. Another 1745 people were deemed to have been "affected" by the development and were also compensated at levels beyond the minimum; 12 took jobs in the company while 86 were given extensive free training to help them into self- employment; 12 households living on the land but without proof titles were also included in these programme. Average annual income is about Rs. 4,000 to 5,000 per month.

5.17.3 Land Acquisition and Displacement for the Refinery

The Lanjigarh refinery is located in a 750-hectare complex. Land acquisition for this refinery was initiated in June 2002 when the Kalahandi district Collector's office sent a letter to affected landowners in 12 villages in the Lanjigarh are, likes, Bundel, Borbhata, Kothadwar, Bandaguda, Sindbaheli, Basantpada, Jagannathpur, Kinari, Kappaguda, Belamba, Boringpaddar and Tiriguda. The letters declared that the district administration intended to compulsory acquire their lands-391 hectares of private land and 628 hectares of common village land-for the Sterlite India's refinery project. The letter also explained that the families to be fully displaced (who would lose their homes in addition to their lands) would be compensated and resettled, while the families, whose lands would be taken over, would be compensated (Letter from NHRC Eastern Region's Special Rapporteur to NHRC, 14 May, 2011).

Vedanta offered the 1,702 families, whose farmlands had been compulsory acquired for the refinery, the option of onetime cash compensation in lieu of employment: initially, 46 families; later 1,372 families received compensation of INR 97.5 million (US $ 1.97 million). There are 1,010ten families preferred not to take cash compensation and sent one person each for technical training at Vedanta's expanse. Of these, 87 individuals completed the training and Vedanta claimed that 11 of them were provided with employments in the refinery. However, it was not clear if the remaining 319 families (who did not take the initial cash offer of send people for technical training) received cash compensation. According to Vedanta officials, 220 of the families had not applied for cash compensations (Letter from NHRC Eastern Region's Special Rapporteur to NHRC, 14 May, 2011).

5.18 REHABILITATION COLONY

The villagers displaced have been rehabilitated in in the Vedanta Rehab colony at the foothills. At the foothills of, the *Niyamgiri (Niyam Dongar)*, there established the Niyamgiri Vedanta Nagar (NVN colony), takes the major attention of the research. In the colony it has all types of facilities such as Health centre, educational institution, marketing facilities, centre for tailoring, water tank, proper drainage system, Anganwadi centre, club house, common latrine, and bath room in the middle of the colony, computer literacy centre, a centre for the DAV International School. However, these facilities are mainly for the company executives while the tribals have been rehabilitated elsewhere. There is a primary school here which is non-functional and was locked in a week day that the survey was conducted. The health centre was also locked.

5.18.1 Resettlement and Rehabilitation Policy

Resettlement and Rehabilitation Policy stated that one member each from fully displaced families would be provided with employment by the company. Vedanta Alunima recently released an information and stated that, as on 1, February, 2009, one person each from 63 of these families has been employed in the refinery and get one person each from the rest of the families had opted for the alternatives available under the policy- a one-time additional cash compensation or technical training towards self-employment (employment details released by Vedanta Aluminium as on 1, February, 2009). Of the 1,220 families from whom farmlands were acquired, this policy states that one person each from the families is to be given priority in employment in the refinery depending on the context of the land acquires out of the family's possession, if this is not feasible, onetime cash assistance, also graded on the context of the land acquired out of the total land in the family's possession.

The tribal group has a symbiotic relationship with the mountain. They practice farming and collect fruits, flowers and fire wood from the forest covers the Niyamgiri. Though the refinery plant is not yet in full operation, it is already threatening this way of life. The land has already been taken from the local communities to build the refinery and black smoke trails from the Chimney (Alumina refinery report, 2005). Sumanta Majhi of Vedanta Nagari rehabilitation colony said, *we have a lot of problems with the sound from the refinery. We are not able to sleep at night. The dust comes into our ears, eyes and hair.*

5.19 IMPACT ON SOCIO-CULTURAL AND RELIGIOUS LIFE

There are two Particularly Vulnerable tribal Groups (PVTGs) in Niyamgiri area. These are the *Kutia Kondhs* who are lives on the plains and the *Dongoria Kondhs* lives in the top of the Niyamgiri hills. There are also to tribal development agencies working for their welfare- for some 35 years. These are the Kutia Kondh development Agency (KKDA), Lanjigarh and the Dongoria Kondh Development Agency (DKDA).

When interviewed the *Dongoria Kondhas* showed deep resentment to the mining proposal on their sacred Niyamgiri hills which they worship. A *Dongoria Kondh* man, explained: "we do not cut down trees on the top of the hill, we will only ever remove some branches if needed, and because we believe that the trees provide shade to *Niyam Raja*. If the company cuts trees at the top of the hills, this would be disastrous for us". Another tribal said, "We do not cultivate at the top of the hill because it supports life in the rest of the hill, if you harm the brain, how will the body work?" (Amnesty International Report, 2010).

The *Dongaria Kondh* also expressed concern about how the mining project would affect their traditional way of life, culture and ability to retain their distinct identity. As reported to Amnesty International a *Dongoria Kondha* mentioned that: *Our language, the way we dress, songs, marriage rituals, worship of Niyam Raja, our livelihoods are also linked to these Hills and the way we live here. We have seen that happens to other Adivasis when they are forced to leave traditional lands, they lose everything.*" Many expressed concern that the impacts of mining on water and forests or the noise and dust from the mine may make it impossible for them to continue to live where they currently do and force them of their hills and traditional lands, another *Dongaria Kondh* man, said, *"our people are not educated. If we are forced to leave these hills because of the mine, we will end up in poorly paid jobs in towns of concrete"*. An elderly woman from Kurlli village stated, *"If we have lakhs or crores of rupees, how many days will it last, but this mountain will last generations"* (Amnesty International Report, 2010). Some of the villagers pointed out that, Niyamgiri is full of pineapple tree, mango trees and jack fruit trees. They are cultivating these fruits since their their forefathers which is sustaining them along with paddy cultivations on the dongars or hill slopes, where *Niyam Raja Penu* is watching us. He will be angry if we will give our land to Vedanta Steel Plant.

5.19.1 Impact of Natural Environment

The mining project also poses risks to the natural environment in the region, which the communities depends on for their own food and livelihoods. The main risks are posed cutting down of forest for the mine site and related infrastructure, noise, blasting and other impacts of the mining operations themselves and management of waste produced as a result of the mining operation.

Due to industrial activities in the area there is an increase of temperature in the to around 40 degree Celsius. Dust from stone blasting has damaged fields and agricultural production. Blasting throws sand and stones on the arable fields and renders them infertile They are thus loosing out on their food and nutrition. Besides, the forests which are a source of minor forest produce and also medicines are being threatened. Water is taken from the river Basundhara and Nagavalli which are the lifeline of the communities is drying up underground reservesbesides getting polluted. Increased temperatures, depleting water resources and pollution along with the threat of loosing agricultural and home lands are threatening tribal lives and existence.

Under these circumstances the tribals will be forced to leave their natural habitats which will affect their soci-economic and cultural practices. They fear their traditional festivals will also be under threat. The company has thus poisoned and damaged the land, water, air and forests of the tribals thereby endangering their right to life.

SECTION-III

5.20 VEDANTA AND DONGORIA KONDHAS

However, the main conflict which has caught world wide attention is the Vedanta's mining lease to mine bauxite for its Lanjigarh complex from the sacred Niyamgiri hills, the home for the Particularly Vulnerable groups (PVT G's) the Dongoria Kondhas. The Dongria Kondhs are a primitive tribe group (PTG) of about 8000, residing in the Niyamgiri hill range stretching in the Rayagada and Kalahandi districts of Odisha (refer map of Odisha). Niyamgiri is an area of densely forested hills and a store house of bauxite. It is named after the mountain god the Niyam Raja. For a decade, however, the Dongria have lived under the threat of mining by Vedanta Resoures, which wants to extract the estimated $2 billion worth of bauxite (aluminium ore) that lies under the surface of the hills. This would prove disastrous and spell the end of the Dongria Kondh as a distinct people. In 2003, before receiving legal clearance to mine, Vedanta built a refinery at the foot of the hills in Lanjigarh. The construction of the refinery forced over a hundred families of Majhi Kondh, a neighboring tribe of the Dongria, to move to a settlement known as 'the rehab colony', where a member of each family has been provided with a job in the refinery.

Vedanta, after making huge investments in the Langigarh plant, it started work on a six-fold expansion of its facilities when gross violations of the Forest Rights Act (2006) were detected. A four member MoEF panel headed by N.C. Sexena, recommended against granting environmental clearance to mining in the Niyamgiri hills.

t recommended "that allowing mining in the proposed nining lease (PML) area, by depriving two primitive ribal groups of their rights over the proposed mining ite inorder to benefit a private company would hake he faith of the tribal people in the law of the land. Since he company has repeatedly violated the law, allowing t further access to the PML area, at the rights of the utia and Dongoria Kondhas, will have serious onsequences for the security and well-being of the entire ountry".

The Kondh villagers report skin problems, livestock iseases and crop damage which they say are due to ollution from the refinery which government inspectors ave described as 'alarming'. The inspectors found that ed mud' — the refinery's main waste product — was eeping, causing contamination of the ground water. Vithout Niyamgiri's bauxite, the company has had ifficulties feeding the refinery, leading to a temporary hutdown in 2012.

In April 2013, in a judgement with important nplications for all of India's tribal peoples, the Supreme ourt ruled that communities affected by the mining roject must be consulted. It asked the Governemnt of disha to seek the consent of the concerned villages as er the provisions of the FRA, 2006 "that primitive tribal roups" have a customary right to worship the mountains nd whether the mining by Vedanta would threaten their eligious rights of worshipping Niyam Raja. However, ne Odisha state government singled out only twelve f more than a hundred Dongria villages in which to onduct the consultations. By August 2013, all 12 Dongria ram sabhas unanimously voted against Vedanta's nining in the Niyamgiri hills. The results of the onsultations are now being considered by India's

Ministry of Environment and Forests, who will have the final say on the mine - but few still believe that the mine will be given the green light. This voting and decision of the gram sabhas would definitely set a precedent for other tribal areas in India.

Pineapple cultivation on Niyamgiri hills, Source: field work, 16-03-2015

Author and Project fellow, with Dongaria Kondh, Niyamgiri hills

Niyamgiri Vedanta Nagar (Vedanta Rehabilitation Colony), Field work, 15-03-2015

Auhor and Project Fellow with Kutia Kondh People of Vedanta Rehabilitaion Colony, 05-05-2015

Author and Project Fellow with Dongoria Kondh Women, Kurli, source: field work, 05-05-2015

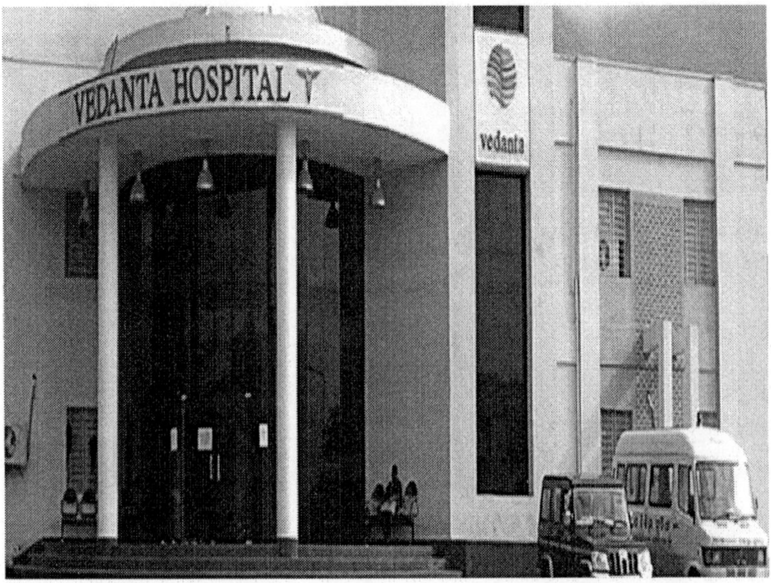

Vedanta Hospital, (Source: field work, 05-05-2015)

DAV Vedanta International School ,source: field work, 05-05-2015

Mid- day meal centre, Lanjigarh, source: field work, 05-05-2015

6

The Way Ahead

The study focussed on three cases of resistance by local communities to the three mega-projects in the State, namely Posco, Vedanta and Tata. What is common in all three is that, the marginalized sections of the society have raised their voices against a "pro-business" state which is forcibly acquiring land from them to support corporate giants.. In the case of Posco, small , marginal farmers, and landless labourers, mostly belonging to scheduled castes are affected by land acquisition. Although, land acquired is mainly government land, the local communities, as cited earlier, have grown betel vines on the government land for generations, because of low agricultural productivity in a cyclone prone area. Betel vine cultivation, being very lucrative and suitable to the climatic conditions, is the main source of livelihood. The forceful demolition of this livelihood has generated immense resentment of the people towards the state and Posco. Finally Posco has had to withdraw from Odisha in 2017 after waiting for over a decade.

Similarly, in the Tata-Kalinganagar project which has started production when the field visit of this study was conducted, generated a lot of attention, when tribal mainly *Mundas,* resisted the acquisition of land, both agricultural and forest lands on which their livelihoods depended. This was met with brute force by the police, resulting in the killing of twelve tribals and a policeman.

Vedanta Project in Lanjigarh, has also been affected by the landmark Supreme Court decision, preventing Vedanta from mining bauxite to feed its Langigarh plant, from the *Niyamgiri* hills, the home of the *dongoria kondhas*. This has been a landmark decision in securing the rights of indigenous population, under the FRA, 2006. The FRA, 2006 has been a major step to "undo the historic injustice" done to the tribals and forest dwellers. Right implementation of this Act will go a long way in ensuring inclusive development in the country.

The three case have highlighted that the western industrialization model is definitely posing a threat to local communities in India. These communities are facing the blunt of capital intensive and resource extractive strategies which are damaging the local indigenous economy.

The government besides threatening the environment is creating more dependency of people on Government support[1] by depriving people off their lands and means of livelihood, rather than building self-sufficiency among the poor and landless.It is ironical that the government on one hand is acquiring land, including agricultural land for industries and SEZs, and on the other hand making the provision of food and employment to the poor an obligation of the state. A self-sufficient rural economy is being damaged wherein *enclosures of dependency* are being generated. The rehabilitation centre that have been created are a far cry from the independent lives the families led while growing their own food. Now one male member of the family is engaged in the industries. This is the case of the *kutia kondhas* in Lanjigarh and also the *Mundas* in Kalinganagar. The women folk who worked in the fields are being forced to look for other alternatives to support the family like selling *handia*, a local drink, commonly witnessed in Kalinganagar.

Therefore, these communities are now getting more and more dependent on the state for food and employment. The Mahatma Gandhi National Rural Employment Guarantee Scheme (*MGNREGS)* has a mandate of providing at least hundred days of guaranteed wage to every rural household, there is a huge gap in reality and practice. In 2019-20, only 1,61, 249 out of 68,45,895 registered households in Odisha had completed hundred days of work, or a meager 2.35% of the rural households (*The Hindu*, April 30, 2020). Further, the schemes are poorly implemented as seen from the field inputs. Thus local communities have to wait for dole outs from the state. Thus, the very people who are supposed to be the beneficiaries of development, are today protesting against these invasive strategies. Thus the question – *what is development and for whom* becomes central to the development discourse? Development is necessary but not at the cost of the poor. Only when it is inclusive and participatory, involving the poor and vulnerable, while protecting their land rights, culture and traditional beliefs, can there be genuine development.

As mentioned in the introduction, Sen refers to development as the process of expansion of real freedom and capabilities that people enjoy, with development strategies focussed on human freedom. It is on this line that this volume concludes that development strategies in India need to recognize the needs and uniqueness of vulnerable sections of the society. Local needs and interests should also be taken into consideration while framing strategies. Therefore there is a need to restructure development policies in building up the capabilities of local communities without threatening indigenous socio-cultural exchanges and livelihoods. An extractive capital centred development shall lead to greater social differentiations and thereby inequalities in the society. Therefore, forceful land acquisition from the vulnerable and poor will push them further into poverty, particularly in a highly agrarian economy like India, where land performs the critical role of providing economic and social security. Such extractive development, as seen from the study, have a devastating effect on the livelihoods and the health of the poor, whereby their right to life is violated.

The present neo-liberal regime has created an exclusionary process of growth that has further marginalized the marginalized. Land laws in India have so far protected the rich farmers and landlords. The RTFCT-LARR, 2013 despite several laudable provisions has failed to check land wars across the country. This has got a push with the LARR

Amendments in 2014,and 2015. The doctrine of *eminent domain* continues to haunt the poor and weaker sections of the society. Section 69 of the Act permits the states to change the purpose for which land has been acquired under "public purpose" clause. Section 70 permits the states to transfer land to private companies and individuals. These empower the states to acquire land under "public purpose". The scope of this clause needs to be reduced. Instead of building self-sufficiency among the poor and land for food, the government is creating more dependents by depriving people off their lands and means of livlihood .It is ironical that the government on one hand is acquiring land, including agricultural land for industries and SEZs, and on the other hand making the obligation of the state towards feeding the poor and hungry ie the poor are first created with a begging bowl and then food is put in that bowl. Industrialization is necessary but not at the cost of grabbing land from the weaker sections of the society. It needs to be balanced with agriculture. Only when it is inclusive and participatory, involving the poor and tribals while protecting their land rights, culture and traditional beliefs can there be genuine development.

"Land to the landless" needs to implemented urgently,either in form of community rights or individual rights. It is a fact that industrial corridors and SEZs cater to the elite and do not support the dispossessed. They are left to fend for themselves or migrate. Kerela has shown that heavy, capital intensive industries are not crucial for growth, a focus on health and education and livelihoods of the poor, is central to economic and social development. It is through this investment in social sectors, along with land reforms which provided deeds to agricultural labourers and land for all that Kerala has successfully lowered poverty[2].

Finally, development strategies, particularly in India, rather than trying to transform the village socio-economies, need to be more place-based, and seek to serve better the needs and desires of the people to enhance their way of life. Local skills and resources need to be harnessed to make communities feel involved in the process. For example the *dongorias* cultivate large quantities of fruits on the slopes of the hills. They sell them in the local weekly market. If food processing plants are set up and the tribals given training in producing jams, jellies, pickels etc the tribal economy is bound to grow. Further, these communities are extremely skilled in making shawls and jewellery. There is a growing market for these products. Through proper guidance and training local communities can integrate their economy with a larger global market . Similar is the case with *paan* cultivation in the disputed site of Posco.

Thus development should be *"socially embedded"* (Polanyi, 1944) rather than being a expanding profit generating market economy dominated by market relations. Building up the capabilities of the poor rather than grabbing their lands, and threatening their livelihoods can bring about equitable growth. Land Acts need to be restructured so that land is not simply considered as a saleable commodity to be compensated in cash. As tribal culture is community driven, the cash is soon exhausted in feasting and drinking,, Buying new land is complex and erratic. Thus the family looses land, employment, food and nutrition.

The health of the entire family suffers economically, socially and also emotionally. The 'one shoe fits all' formula is no longer acceptable and will only create resistance to projects under a neo-liberal regime. Thus *"socially embedded"* strategies will help build capabilities and increase local participation and inclusion thereby reducing state-society conflicts.

NOTES

1. For instance, the Government's Employment Generation Scheme (the Mahatama Gandhi Employment Generation Scheme) which is aimed to provide 100 days of employment to the poor (for details – refer to the Planning Commission of India – www.planningcommission.nic.in). Also the National Food Security Act (NFSA, 2013).
2. One step in this direction is the present Government's emphasis on skill development through its Make-in-India program. But this is a new policy and its impact is still to be felt.

Bibliography

A Haroon Akram-Lodhi (2007) "Land, Markets and Neoliberal Enclosure: An Agrarian Political Economy Perspective". *Third World Quarterly*, 28:8, 1437-1456.

Asher, Manshi (2009): 'Striking While the Iron is Hot: A Case study of Pohang Steel Company (POSCO)'s Proposed Project in Orissa, National Centre for Advocacy Studies, Pune, India.

Ali Haruna, Felix Aromo Ilesanmi and Bukar Dip Yerima (2013) "Problems of Formal Land Acquisition Policies in Nigeria: The Case of Jimeta-Yola, Adamawa State, Nigeria". *Journal of Environment and Earth Science*, Vol. 3, No. 11.

Bandyopadhyay, J (2003) 'And Quiet Flows the River project', *The Hindu Business Line,* March 14.

Banerjee, Sumanta (2012) Revolutionary Movements in a Post-Marxian Era *Economic and Political Weekly*.Vol. XLII no. 18, May, 5, 2012, pp. 55-61.

Bardhan, B., Kaushik. B., Choudhury, M., Ghatk, M., Guha, A., Majumdar, M., Mookharjee, D and Roy, D (2007) Industrial in West Bengal, *Economic and Political Weekly*. April, 28, pp. 1487-1489.

Bardhan, Pranab (1984). *The Political Economy of India's Development*, Oxford University Press, Oxford.

Baxi, U. (2008), "Development, Displacement and Resettlement: A Human Right Perspective" *Indian Social Development Report*. CSD, Oxford.

Bharati, I. (1991), "Bihar's Dam, Tribals Woes", *Economic and Political Weekly*, 1, June.

Ben White, Saturnino M. Borras Jr., Ruth Hall, Ian Scoones & Wendy Wolford (2012): "The New Enclosures: Critical Perspectives on Corporate Land Deals", *Journal of Peasant Studies*, 39:3-4, 619-647.

Bhagawati, Jagadish (2004) *In Defence of Globalization*, Oxford University Press, Oxford.

Bhagawati, Jagadish (1993) *India in Transition: Freeing the Economy* (Oxford: Clarendon Press).

Bernstein, Henry(2010). *Class Dynamics of Agrarian Change: Agrarian Change and Peasant Studies Series*, Firewood Publishing, Halifax and Winnipeg.

Ben White, Saturnino M. Borras Jr., Ruth Hall, Ian Scoones & Wendy Wolford (2012): "The new enclosures: critical perspectives on corporate land deals", *Journal of Peasant Studies*, 39:3-4, 619-647.

Borras Jr., Saturnino M. , Hall, Ruth , Scoones, Ian , White, Ben and Wolford, Wendy(2011) "Towards a better understanding of global land grabbing: an editorial introduction", *Journal of Peasant Studies*, 38: 2, 209 — 216

Bose, Sugata and Ayesha Jajal (ed.) (2011, 11th Impression), *Nationalism, Democracy and Development: State and Politics in India*, Oxford University Press, Oxford, New Delhi

Borras Jr., Saturnino M., Hall, Ruth, Scoones, Ian, White, Ben and Wolford, Wendy (2011) "Towards a better understanding of global land grabbing: an editorial introduction", *Journal of Peasant Studies,* 38: 2, pp. 209-216.

Central Empowered Committee, Report in IA No. 1324. Regarding the Alumina Refinery Plant being set up by M/S Vedanta Alumina Limited at Lanjigarh in Kalahandi district, Orissa, 21, September, 2005.

Chandhoke, N. (2006) "Peoples Movement and the Articulation of Rights", *Indian Journal of Human Rights,* Vol.10&11, No. 1&2, Jan-Dec.

Corbridge, Stuart (2009) "The Political Economy of Development in India since Independence", Development Studies Institute, London School of Economics, London.

Das, Raju (2014) 'India in Crisis', *Canadian Dimension,* March-April, 48, 2 : 46.

Daspatnaik P.1984, *Adivasi* (Journal of the Harijan and Tribal Research Institute, January Bhubaneswar).

Development Induced Displacement of the Adivasis, State of the Adivasis in Odisha 2014. A Human Development Analysis, Sage Publications India Pvt Ltd.

Dev, Mahendra S. (ed.) *Indian Development Report 2012-13,* Oxford University Press, New Delhi.: 2013, pp 233-246.

Dipak Ghosh (2007) The metamorphosis of Lewis's dual economy model. *Journal of Economic Methodology,* 14:1, 5-25.

Dixit, Anita (2013) "Agrarian Poverty, Nutrition and Economic Class of Gujarat, India",. *Journal of Agrarian Change,* vol 13, no 2, April: 263-281.

Dreze, Jean and Amartya Sen (2013). *An Uncertain Glory: India and its Contradictions.* Allen Lane (Penguin), London.

——— (2002). *India: Development and Participation*, Oxford University Press, New Delhi.

——— (1998) *India: Economic Development and Participation*, Oxford University Press, New Delhi.

——— ed., (1997). *Indian Development: Selected Regional Perspectives*, Oxford University Press, New Delhi.

Easton, David (1981) *The Political System: An Inquiry into the State of Political Science* (Chicago: University of Chicago Press, Chicago.

Ekka, A and Mohammed, A (2000): *Development and Induced Displacement and Rehabilitation in Jharkhand: A data base on its Extent and Nature*, Indian Social Institute, New Delhi.

Evers, Sandra J.T.M, Caroline Seagal and Froukje Krijtenburg (eds) 2013. *Africa for Sale: Positioning the state, Land and Society in Foreign Large-Scale Land Acquisition in Africa*. Brill, Leiden, Boston.

Fernandes, Walter (1994). *Development Induced Displacement in the Tribal Areas of Eastern India*, pp.24, ISI, New Delhi. (Mimeo)

——— (1998): Development-Induceed Displacement in Eastern India' in S.C Dube (ed.) *Antiquity to Modernity in Tribal India*, Inter India Publications, New Delhi. pp. 217-301.

Fernandes, W and Mohammed Asif (1997): *Development-Induced Displacement in Orissa 1951 to 1995: A data base on its Extent and Nature*, India Social Institute, New Delhi.

Fernandes, W and Niraj Naik (2001): *Development and Induced-displacement in Goa 1965-1995: A Study on its Extent and Nature*. India Social Institute, New Delhi.

Frankel. R, Francine (2005) *India's Political Economy, 1947-2004: the Gradual Revolution*.

Fernandes, W. (2007), Singur and Displacement Scenario, .*Economic and Political Weekly*, Vol.42, No.3, Jan. 20-26, pp. 203-206.

GOI, (1996) The Panchayats (Extension to Scheduled Areas) (also called PESA or Tribal Self- Rule Law) Act, 1996, New Delhi.

Government of India (GOI) (2011) Census of India, New Delhi.

——— (2011) *Odisha: District Census Handbook, Jagatsinghpur,* Series 22, Part XXB, Directorate of Census, Operations, Odisha.

——— (2006) The Scheduled Tribes and Other Traditional Forest Dwellers (Recognition of Forest Rights) Act 2006.

——— (2013), The Right to Fair Compensation and Transparency in Land Acquisition, Rehabilitation and Resettlement (RCFCT-LARR,) Act, 2013.

——— Special Economic Zones in India, Ministry of Commerce and Industries, New Delhi (http:// sezindia.nic.in/ (accessed 1 March 2014).

—— (2013) National Food Security Act, 2013 (NFSA).

Govt. of Orissa (GoO) Orissa Scheduled Areas Transfer of Immovable Property (by Scheduled Tribes), Regulation, 2 of 1956.

——— (1960), Orissa Land Reform (O.L.R) Act 1960).

——— (2002), (Letter No. 205 (400)dt 6.6.2002, Office of the District Collector, Kalahandi, at Bhawanipatna.

——— (2003), Minerals resources in Orissa and India-2002-03, Directorate of Geology, Orissa.

——— (2011), District Statistical Handbook, *Kalahandi,* Directorate of Economics and Statistics, Odisha, Bhubaneswar.

——— (2011) District Statistical Handbook, *Jajpur*, Directorate of Economics and Statistics, Odisha, Bhubaneswar

——— (2011) Letter from NHRC Eastern Region's Special Rapporteur to NHRC, 14 May.

——— (2014-15) *Economic Survey of Odisha*, Dept of Planning and Coordination, Government of Odisha

Odisha District Gazetteers, *Jagatsinghpur.*, Gopobandhu Academy of Administration, Government of Odisha.

Odisha District Gazetteers, *Jajpur*, Gopobandhu Academy of Administration, Government of Odisha.

Odisha District Gazetteers, *Kalahandi*, Gopobandhu Academy of Administration , Government of Odisha.

Gupta, Akhil and K.Sivaramakrishnan,ed. (2010) The State in India after Liberalization: Interdisciplinary Perspectives, Rutledge, London.

Hirway, Indira (2012), Inclusive Growth under a Neo-Liberal framework, *EPW*, Vol. XLII no. 18, May, 5, pp55-61.

Harvey, David (2005), *A Brief History of Neo-liberalism*, Oxford University Press, New York.

——— (2003). *The New Imperialism*, Oxford University Press, Oxford.

Hall, Derek, Phillip Hirsch, Tanya Murray Li (2011). *Powers of Exclusion in Southeast Asia.* National University of Singapore Press (NUS), Singapore.

Hirway, Indira(2000). "Dynamics of Development in Gujarat: Some Issues." *EPW*, vol 35, no. 35/36, August 26:pp.3106-20.

Ian Scoones, Ruth Hall, Saturnino M. Borras Jr, Ben White & Wendy Wolford (2013) "The politics of evidence: Methodologies for understanding the global land rush", *The Journal of Peasant Studies*, 40:3, 469-483.

Jena, Debendra and Kar, M (2012), "Social Cost of Development: A Study on displacement and Resettlement of the Tribals Affected under Mahindra Dasm Project. Indira Gandhi Rastriya Manv Sangrhalaya, Bhopal, Madhya Pradesh.

Katzenstein, Mary, Smitu Kothari, and Uday Mehta (2001). Social Movement Politics in India." in Atul Kohli, ed., *The Success of India' Democracy,* Cambridge University Press,

Kohli, Atul (2012). *Poverty amid Plenty in the New India,* Cambridge University Press, Cambridge.

——— (2010) *Democracy, and Development in India: From Socialism to Pro-Business,* OUP, New Delhi.

——— (2004), *State-directed Development: Political Power and Industrialization in the Global Periphery,* Cambridge University Press, Cambridge.

Kothari, S. (2006), "Whose Nation? The Displaced as Victims of Development".*Economic and Political Weekly.* Vol: 31, No.24, June.

Kay, Sylvia (2014). Policy Shift: Investing in Agricultural Alternatives, Transnational Institute for Hands off the Land Alliance, The Netherlands.

Levian, M (2013a). "Regimes of Dispossession: From Steel Towns to Special Economic Zones". *Development and Change,* 44(2): 381-407

——— (2012a). "The Politics of Dispossession: Theorizing India's ''Land Wars'. *Politics and Society* 41:351

——— (2012b) "The land Question: Special Economic Zones and the Political Economy of Dispossession in India", *The Journal of Peasant Studies,* 39:3-4, 933-969.

——— (2011) "Special Economic Zones and accumulation by dispossession in India". *Journal of Agrarian Change,* Vol. 11, No. 4: pp. 454–483.

Li, Tanya Murray (2009). "To Make Live or Let Die?Rural Dispossession and the Protection of Surplus Populations". *Antipode.* vol. 41, Issue Supplement S1 January, pp: 66-93.

——— (2007). *The Will to Improve: Governmentality, Development, and the Practice of Politics,* Duke University Press, Durham and London.

Lasgorcelx, A and Kothari, A. (2009): "Displacement and Relocation of Protected Ares: A Synthesis and Analysis of Case Studies." *Economic and Political Weekly,* Vol. 44. No. 49 (December 5-11), pp. 37-47.

Lewis, Arthur W.(1977). *The Evolution of International Economic Order,* Princeton University Press, Princeton.

Mohapatra, L.K. (1991) "Development for whom?" Depriving The Displaced Tribal's, *Social Action.* July-November, pp. 88-91.

Majhi, U.N.(2009), 'Tribal Land Alienation: Needs Radical Solution' in Ota, A.B ed. (2009), *Critical Issues in Tribal Development,* SC & ST Research and Training Intitute, Bhubaneswar.

Miliband, Ralph (1969). The State in Capitalist Society. Basic Books, New York.

Memorandum of Understanding between the Government of Orissa and M/s POSCO for establishment of an integrated steel plant at Paradeep, (available at http:/ / www.orissa.gov.in/ posco/POSCO MoU.htm.).

http://www.forestrightact.com/component/article/21/87-timeline-of-events-relating to forest right.in POSCO area.

Menon, M. (2003): *Large Dam for Hydropower in North-East India: A Dossier,* Kalpavrish, Pune.

Mishra, S (2009), *Poverty and Agrarian Distress in Orissa,* Indira Gandhi Institute of Development Research, Mumbai, September.

Mishra, Aparajita (2010) "The impact of Kalinga Nagar Industrial Complex on Livelihood and Culture of the tribal Communities in Jajpur district, Odisha". Indira Gandhi Rastriya Manv Sangrhalaya, Bhopal, Madhya Pradesh-462013.

Misra, Banikanta and Sagarika Mishra(2014) "Mining and Industrialization: dangerous Portents". *EPW, Vol. XLIX, April 5:56-65.*

Mishra, Swasat, K. (2012) "Industrialization and Displacement in Kalinga Nagar: A Case study of Tata Steel Paribar Colony. *Social Change,* .January, Vol. 26, No.3, pp. 306-309.

Mohanty, Manoranjan (2014).""Persisting Dominance: Crisis of Democracy in a Resource–rich Region". *EPW, Vol. XLIX, April 5:39-45.*

Mohanty, R. (2011). Impact of Development Project on the Displaced Tribals: A Case Study of a Development Project in Eastern India. *Orissa Review.* September-October, pp-67-73.

Mohanty, B.B (2001), Land Distribution Among Scheduled Caste and Scheduled Tribe, *EPW,* vol. 36, No. 40, Oct 6-12, pp 3857-3868.

Morris, Sebastian and Ajay Pandey(2007). Towards Reform of Land Acquisition Framework", *EPW,* vol. 42, no.22, June 2: 2083-2090.

MoU, Memorandum of Understanding between the Government of Odisha and M/S Posco for establishment of An Integrated Steel plant at Paradeep available at (http://www.orissa.gov.in/posco/Posc MoU.htm)

Mukhopadhyay, A.D. (2006): "The POSCO Deal: Boon or Disaster"? *Social Scientist,* Vol. 34, No. 3/4 (Mar. - Apr., 2006), pp. 43-54.

Nandy, Ashis, The Political Culture of the Indian State in Hasan, Zoya ed (2009 Edition), *Politics and the State in India,* Sage Publications, New Delhi, pp. 64-88.

Nayyar, Deepak (1998), 'Economic Development and Political Democracy: Interactions of Economics and Politics in Independent India', *EPW,* Vol 33, no. 49, Dec 5-11, pp. 3121-3131.

Oskarsson, Patrik (2013). "Dispossession by Confusion from Mineral-Rich Lands in Central India, South Asia", *Journal of South Asian Studies*, 36:2, 199-212.

Ota, A. (2010) *Displacement and Rehabilitation Issues in Tribal Areas- A diagnostic Analysis,* Inter-India Publications (IIP), pp : 24-25.

Ota, A. (2009), *Development and Induced displacement and the tribals,* Scheduled Caste and Scheduled Tribes Research and Training Institute, Orissa, Bhubaneswar.

Padel, Felix (2001). *The Sacrifice of human being: British Rule and the Khonds of Orissa,* Oxford University Press, New Delhi.

Padel, Felix and Samarendra Das (2010). *Out of This Earth: East India Adivasis and the Aliminium Cartel,* Orient Blackswan, New Delhi.

Panagariya, Arvind (2008). *India: The Emerging Giant*, OUP, New York.

Parsons, Talcott and Edward Shils (1951) *Toward a General Theory of Action* (Cambridge, MA: Harvard University Press.

Patnaik, Prabhat (1999). "The Performance of the Indian Economy," *Social Scientist*, vol.27, nos. 5-6 (May-June, pp. 3-16.

Patnaik, Utsa ed. (1990). *Agrarian Relations and accumulation: The Mode of Production Debate in India,* OUP, Bombay.

Patnaik, S (2001) Myth and Reality of Devolution of Power, An Examination of PESA in Orissa, Draft Paper for the CIFOR Research Project on 'Creating Space for Local Forest Management', Bhubaneswar.

Rajni Kothari (2005), *Rethinking Democracy,* Orient Longman, New Delhi.

Ranis, Gustav (2004)." The Evolution of Development Thinking: Theory and Practice : *Centre Discussion Paper No. 886*, Yale University Press.

Ray, Raka and Mary Katzenstein(2005). *Social Movements in India,* Rowman and Little field, Oxford.

Rudolf, Lloyd and Susanne Rudolf (1987), In Pursuit of Laxmi. University of Chicago Press, Chicago.

Rupavath, Ramdas (2009). *Tribal Land Alienation and Political Movements: Socio-economic Patterns from South,* Cambridge Scholars, New Castle.

Sahu, Geetanjoy (2008) "Mining in the Niyamgiri Hills"., *Economic and Political Weekly,* Vol. 43, No. 15 (April 12-18), pp. 19-21.

Sarin, Madhu, Neera M. Singh, Nandini Sundar and Ranu K. Bhogal (2003) *Devolution as a Threat to Democratic to Decision-making in Forestry? Findings from Three States in India,* Overseas Development Institute, London, UK.

Schumpeter, Joseph, A (2003 edn), *Capitalism, Socialism and Democracy,* Routledge, London, New York.

Sharma, R.N. (2003), "Involuntary Displacement: A Few Encounters". *Economic and Political Weekly,* Vol.38, No.09, pp. 907-912.

Shrama, R.N. and Singh S.R., (2009) "Displacement in Singrauli Region: Entitlements and rehabilitation", *Economic and Political Weekly,* Vol -XLV, No-51, pp. 62-67, December.

Sampat, Preeti (2013), Limits to Absolute Power: Eminent Domain and the Right to Land in India, *Economic and Political Weekly,* Vol. XLVIII, No.19, May 11, pp. 40-52.

Sampat, P., (2008) 'Special Economic Zones in India'. *Economic and Political Weekly*, 43: (28): 25–30.

Satapathy, Rajaram (2013). 'Mines Multiply as Farmland Shrinks', *The Times of India*, Bhubaneswar, 22 February

Sen, Amartya (1999). *Development as Freedom,* Oxford University Press, New Delhi.

Shah, Ghanshyam(ed), 2002. *Social Movements and the State,* Sage, New Delhi.

Stiglitz, Joseph (2002) *Globalization and its Discontents.* WW Norton and Company, New York.

Swapna Banerjee-Guha (2013) "Accumulation and Dispossession: Contradictions of Growth and Development in Contemporary India, South Asia." *Journal of South Asian Studies,* 36:2, 165-179.

UNDP, (2008), *Status Report : Land Rights and Ownership in Orissa,* UNDP, India.

UNDP Human Development Report (2016), *Human Development for Everyone,* UNDP, New York (available at http://hdr.undp.org/en/statistics/)

Wendy Wolford, Saturnino M. Borras Jr.,Ruth Hall, Ian Scoones and Ben White (2013), Governing Global Land Deals: The Role of the State in the Rush for Land. *Development and Change* 44(2): 189–210.

World Bank (2003). *Land Policies for Growth and Poverty. Oxford University Press,* Oxford.

■■■■